T0128214

This book is dedicated to the 4 most important women in my life:
To my daughter Rebecca, who is a constant joy
and makes me proud to be her Dad,
To my sister Vera, who keeps me honest and
never lets me get too big headed,
To my life partner Shayla, who lovingly helps
edit my writing and my life and
To my niece Anna, The California girl, who
will probably turn out to be a better
writer than I ever will.

RISING UP FROM HURT

Uncommon Strategies To Develop
Resilience And Rise Above Adversity

Dr. Tom Steiner

Alpha Coach
January 2017

authorHOUSE®

AuthorHouse™
1663 Liberty Drive
Bloomington, IN 47403
www.authorhouse.com
Phone: 1 (800) 839-8640

© 2017 Dr. Tom Steiner. All rights reserved.

No part of this book may be reproduced, stored in a retrieval system, or transmitted by any means without the written permission of the author.

Published by AuthorHouse   01/12/2017

ISBN: 978-1-5246-5872-4 (sc)
ISBN: 978-1-5246-5870-0 (hc)
ISBN: 978-1-5246-5871-7 (e)

Library of Congress Control Number: 2017900183

Print information available on the last page.

Any people depicted in stock imagery provided by Thinkstock are models, and such images are being used for illustrative purposes only. Certain stock imagery © Thinkstock.

This book is printed on acid-free paper.

Because of the dynamic nature of the Internet, any web addresses or links contained in this book may have changed since publication and may no longer be valid. The views expressed in this work are solely those of the author and do not necessarily reflect the views of the publisher, and the publisher hereby disclaims any responsibility for them.

Contents

Chapter 1

HOW HAVE YOU DEALT WITH YOUR HURT?

Connie is an extraordinarily busy, outgoing, successful young woman. On the surface, everything in her life seems to be going very well. However, no matter how hard she tries to find the right relationship, she never seems to connect with the right person. Other people think she's got it made, but Connie isn't so sure.

Jimmy succeeds at almost everything he does. He was a star athlete in school. Now he is a successful businessman and the envy of all of his friends. The only person he can't seem to please is his father, who always expects "only the best" from Jimmy. While he has an incredible list of accomplishments, Jimmy wonders why he isn't happy much of the time.

Monte prides himself on being an "early adopter." He is always the first among his friends to buy and show off the newest gadget and technology. He thinks of himself as being "on the cutting edge." However, he also has built up a significant amount of debt on his credit cards. Monte isn't quite sure how he will pay off these debts.

What do these 3 people have in common? As you get to know them better, you will see that each of them has suffered considerable hurt in the past. Because they have not dealt with their hurt effectively, they continue to carry it with them daily. This hurt controls decisions they make and feelings that they have, regardless of how the situation may look from the outside

Are YOUR past hurts controlling some of YOUR current behaviors?

Hurt hurts. It can be a momentary sting of pain, an emotional anesthetic or it can stop you dead in your tracks. However, it can also become the clarion call for you to consider changing the way you live. It can be the catalyst you need to jump-start your life and move you forward with renewed vigor and energy.

You will get hurt at times in your life. That is a given. It could be a little bit. It could be a lot. It may seem unfair or even unbearable at times. No matter what force you feel drives the universe, be it G-d, karma, fate, luck of the draw or random happenstance, you will receive your designated share of hurt.

You also know that when you are hurt, the pain can feel overwhelming and frightening. You feel that your hurt is unique and personal and that no one else can possibly imagine how much hurt you are experiencing.

But what if I told you that IT IS WHAT YOU DO AFTER YOU GET HURT THAT MATTERS THE MOST? The way in which you perceive and "reframe" your hurt will determine how much it controls your behavior today and into the future.

If you're not convinced, try this. Think of one betrayal or major disappointment in a key relationship (with a parent, lover, colleague or friend) in your life. Remember that awful feeling you associated with that event? What was your reaction?

Did you:
1) Become distrustful or skeptical when new people attempted to engage with you?
2) Allow the hurt to become an emotional anchor attached to your soul?
3) Freeze that feeling of hurt into your consciousness?
4) Swear that you would not allow anyone to treat you that way again?
5) Build emotional walls to insulate yourself?
6) Refuse to stick your toes too far into the emotional pool again?
7) Swap the potential for joy in order to protect yourself from the prospect of hurt?
8) Accept that dull, achy, empty feeling inside you as collateral damage for this protection?
9) Think that once the trauma was gone, the hurt would disappear as well?

As a current pop psychologist might ask, "How's that working for you?" The sad answer for many people just like you is that it is not working. Some of those people are seeking a better way to handle their past hurt.

Are you ready for a new outlook?

The key element is that you have choices, and the choices are UP TO YOU. While you can't change the course of history/events that you interpret as hurtful, you can choose to modify your reaction to those events. This process is called "reframing." You can allow hurt to control your life and limit your options or you can rise up from your hurt.

How?

Realize that your hurt is real, and one way or another you HAVE TO DEAL WITH IT.

Here's the secret—

How YOU CHOOSE to recognize, reframe and deal with your hurt in the short run will determine how happy YOU will be in the long run. There are usually several options to deal with your hurt, each with its own unique set of benefits, challenges and consequences.

This book will guide you along a process of 15 steps through which you will learn to "reframe your hurt." The following steps do not have to be followed in order.

1) Understand how you have dealt with your hurt in the past by identifying old scripts that you have created and understanding how they impact your SELF CONCEPT,
2) Identify how to effectively process your deep feelings of hurt and then CAREFRONT them,
3) Understand how your brain deals with feelings of hurt,
4) Define the issue that is causing your hurt in at least 3 ways,
5) Understand the "payoffs/benefits" you accrue by choosing to stay hurt,
6) Understand the "payoffs/benefits" you will get for rising up from your hurt,
7) Identify if you are stuck in a behavioral rut and learn how to get "unstuck,"
8) Create a sense of urgency to motivate you to take action today,
9) Identify factors that will help you choose options to rise up from your hurt,
10) Identify 3-5 options to rise up from your hurt,
11) Identify questions that will help you challenge your assumptions and "reframe" your issue,

12) Overcome Fear of Failure by Identifying small successful steps to help you rise up from your hurt,

13) Create an action plan to rise up from your hurt,

14) Stay on track when new hurts and relapses occur,

15) Live the fulfilling life you were meant to live.

Let's look at it from another perspective.

Isaac Newton's First Law of Motion is straightforward. Simply put, it states: "An object at rest tends to stay at rest AND an object in motion tends to stay in motion with the same speed and direction UNLESS ACTED UPON BY AN UNBALANCED FORCE." Then the object can move in a very different manner at a very different speed. Too bad, he restricted his theories to objects, because people behave in EXACTLY THE SAME WAY.

People who get "STUCK" in their hurt tend to stay "STUCK" in that hurt or continue to engage in the same behaviors that led them to getting STUCK in the first place. They do this because they rarely attempt to "reframe" the hurt or understand the payoffs/benefits that they derive from hurting. Plus, they don't see other options to reframe the hurt. They find it easier and safer to stay STUCK, rather than to risk unknown hurt and failure from trying something new, courageous or different.

Once a person accepts being STUCK, it is unlikely that they will act quickly and decisively to solve their problem UNLESS ACTED UPON BY AN UNBALANCED FORCE. In fact, common sense definitions of futility tend to focus on the notion of "continuing to do the same things over and over again while expecting different results."

This book can help you to identify and recognize your hurt. It will also show you the benefits/payoffs that you receive for "hanging on to your hurt." More importantly, it will show you a method to think differently and find less painful alternatives to consider.

This book can be YOUR UNBALANCED FORCE. It can show you how to deal with your hurt. It can help you to never allow yourself to get STUCK again!

What this book CAN DO:

1) Provide you with insights about your level of hurt.

2) Provide you with insights about how you got stuck maintaining the hurt.

3) Provide you with insights about how to get unstuck.
4) Become the UNBALANCED FORCE in your life to help you start fully living and being happier again.

What this book CAN'T DO:
1) Take your hurt away for you. You have to do that.
2) Provide you with all the confidence and skill that you need, so that you won't feel any fear, hurt or uncertainty. Learning to deal with hurt and fear is a necessary part of the process.
3) Provide the answer to every problem (Some hurt is the result of very complicated situations. Some hurt is related to things that you had absolutely no control or choice about.)

Who SHOULD NOT READ THIS BOOK?
1) People who think they have all the answers (or don't even ask the questions.)
2) People who want to continue to be STUCK.
3) People who would rather think, read, pray or wish that things would change.
4) People who are looking for sympathy for having the problem.
5) People who think whining will help more than taking action.
6) People who aren't ready to deal with their hurt.

Who SHOULD READ THIS BOOK?
1) People who are tired of being STUCK.
2) People who are ready to change the way they live their lives, stop hurting and start being happier.
3) People who want to live life to the fullest.

So who are YOU today? Mired in a "pity party" Perpetually feeling like a victim? Sick and tired of spinning your wheels and getting nowhere fast?

Is this the perfect time for YOU to rise up from YOUR hurt and do something radically different?

The choice is yours. Will you continue to remain stuck and allow past hurts to invade your future or are you willing to consider that your hurt can be "reframed" to become a meaningful event that can impel and motivate you to change for the better?

Chapter 2

DO YOU OWN YOUR HURT?

Everyone I know has problems today. All different kinds of problems. Some people don't have enough money. Others don't have enough time to do what they want. Some are in the wrong relationship or in no relationship at all. Others haven't lived up to their own or someone else's expectations. Some aren't living the life they expected to live. Others are too stressed out to do much of anything. What do all of these people (and maybe YOU) have in common? 3 things.

First, they are all hurting. Some people are consciously aware of their hurt every day. Some people are largely unaware of their hurt. To cope with their feelings (which can range from vague discomfort or emptiness to angst and sleepless nights), they engage in a variety of behaviors which only temporarily mask the hurt. Some hide it. Some bury it and cover it up by staying busy or getting overly involved in something else. Others turn to drugs, alcohol, sex or even shopping in order to mask the hurt. But the hurt is there and it drives their behavior in a destructive way. Big Time.

Second, they don't own any of the hidden payoffs/benefits that they are receiving for maintaining their current behaviors. Some may not even acknowledge that there are any hidden payoffs/benefits. They simply keep moving along; believing that they are just coping as well as they can in their current situation. Often, they choose not to deal directly with their hurt.

Therefore, the problem is NOT handled in an efficient way or at the optimal time. By the time they finally do decide to deal with the hurt, it is usually long overdue. In somewhat of a "self-fulfilling prophecy," they are now overloaded with hurt or feel like they are in an emergency situation. They feel flooded with angry or hurtful thoughts. Clearly not the best time to deal with problems. In fact, it is one of the worst times to deal with problems. In the long run, this causes them to hang on to their pain and HURT longer, instead of becoming happier.

Third, they often don't deal effectively with the hurt. Many people choose not to deal with their hurt at all. They imagine that the hurt they will have to face if they change their situation will be enormous and intolerable. Unknown hurt always seems greater than known hurt. They assume that the hurt associated with changing their situation is always greater than what they are currently experiencing. The truth is that if their hurt is "CAREFRONTED" during a relatively early stage or in a more optimal fashion, the actual level of hurt could be reduced, allowing the person to experience real happiness.

Are YOU doing this? No?

CONNIE

Remember Connie? Connie didn't think she was doing this either. Some people act like they don't have a care in the world. Connie was one of those people. At 34, she was bright, attractive, financially well off and surrounded by people all of the time. There was rarely a moment in her schedule that was not filled with her job, tennis, theater, family or friends. She was the "life of the party" at social events and was surrounded by many women who envied her "jet set" life.

She was busy ALL of the time. While she was constantly approached for dates by many eligible men, she was rather distant in her approach to "starting a relationship." Though she could have had her pick of the litter, Connie rarely saw anyone more than a handful of times. There was always "something missing" from their encounters.

Was Connie hurting? She didn't think so. She could afford to be selective and was convinced that "Mr. Right" was waiting out there for her. He probably is, but THERE IS NO WAY in the world that he'd have half a chance with Connie, no matter how amazing he is, until she is willing to deal with her hidden pain.

Connie's father had died when she was only a teenager. He died suddenly in a car accident on the way home from work. One morning he was smiling at her and within 2 days, she was sobbing at his funeral. At the same time, Connie's high school sweetheart, Robbie, (the only guy she dated at all, for her first three years of high school) met another girl, while working at his summer job. Unexpectedly, Robbie got her pregnant and quickly married her before they graduated.

Connie grieved a little but then threw herself into a life where she was constantly on the go. Connie didn't see the connection. Do you?

The reason Connie was so busy all of the time was to avoid being flooded with pain and thoughts about being abandoned and left alone. As long as she was busy and constantly "on the go," it was easy for her to see her life as productive and relatively stress free. After all, everyone wanted to be with her. Many wanted to be like her. As long as she didn't allow herself much time alone to think, she was fine.

As far as men were concerned, there was no reason to let a man get too close to her, since they'd just leave anyway. That was the script that had been written early in her life by two of the most important men she had ever known. Weren't all other men likely to do the same? Wasn't it just the nature of the beast?

Connie never bothered to think about this script, but it now dictated how she lived her life years later. "Mr. Right" would never get a chance to get to know Connie. She kept all of the potential men in her life at a distance. She would not let herself be open to these men emotionally or physically for at least 6 months. She reasoned that most of these men were simply looking for "easy sex." It was clear to her that they had to "prove themselves" to her, before any connectivity was going to happen. It was more likely the case that Connie wasn't going to allow anyone to disrupt the life she had set up, the life that masked the pain of the hurt that she still held onto after all of these years.

Most of the men she dated, resented the amount of energy it took to get nowhere with Connie, quickly gave up and moved on. This sad cycle only served to validate to Connie that she was right in the first place, for being so "selective." Men are just "pigs with shoes on." They just leave. That is their nature. She never considered or owned her part in this process.

Let's face it. People do leave your life at times. Some people leave willfully, while others are taken from us. When this occurs, it can be a very hurtful experience. We can try to "insulate ourselves" from further hurt by getting involved with other people or things or by staying busy or not allowing new people to get too close to us. But does that really result in living a "happy life?"

When I asked Connie if she was hurting, her quick response was "No." She was surprised that I even asked such a silly question. She was also surprised that I wasn't impressed with all of her activities and accomplishments. When I asked Connie who she was, she told me about the activities she did. When I asked her who she was underneath all of the activities, she didn't have a quick answer because she really didn't know.

Do YOU know who YOU ARE? Connie's self-concept was more concerned with her activities and accomplishments than with who she was as a person.

Connie hadn't spent a lot of time thinking about who she really was. She thought it was a waste of time. It was so much easier to define herself by her hobbies, interests and her job. When she did have time to herself, she would quickly call or text one of her friends to plan an activity. Connie never gave herself enough time to really consider whether or not she was really "happy" or "just busy."

Like most people, Connie didn't possess a straightforward tool to help her see the underlying pain from different perspectives and to find options to relieve or eliminate the pain. At first she didn't even think there was a problem.

It took a while for Connie to understand that her whole life revolved around staying busy, usually surrounded by other people, so that she wouldn't have to deal with her fears of being abandoned and left alone AGAIN.

It took a while for Connie to understand that her whole life revolved around staying busy, usually surrounded by other people, so that she wouldn't have to deal with her fears of being abandoned and left alone AGAIN.

I am not sure what happened to Connie. Left to her own devices it was always easier for her to just get and stay busy than to deal with her past. Perhaps as she gets older, she may be more willing to open herself up to the excitement and possibilities of a new and exciting relationship

Other people with more awareness of their hurt find themselves stuck between the proverbial ROCK and HARD PLACE. Many have adopted a variety of submissive attitudes such as:

1) "It isn't that bad; others have it worse."
2) "Nothing can be done about it."
3) "Grin and bear it." (the stiff upper lip stance)
4) "Rub dirt on it."
5) "Maybe someone else will do something about it." or "Something else will happen so, that I don't have to do anything about it." (delusions of magical intervention)

These attitudes and others like them serve to keep people running, some rather frantically, in place on the "treadmill of continual suffering."

It does not have to be that way. Many people described in this book have risen up from their hurt and are now enjoying a happier and more productive life. Which approach would be better for you?

Chapter 3

FEELING YOUR FEELINGS AND THEN CAREFRONTING THEM

When events occur that evoke feelings of fear or hurt, you have many choices about how to deal with those feelings. You can deal with them at a surface level. You can choose (consciously or unconsciously) to avoid or postpone dealing with them or dig deeper and truly process your feelings. The critical issue is that your hurt will remain with you, although you may not be aware of it, until you work through your feelings completely.

DEALING WITH YOUR FEELINGS AT A SURFACE LEVEL

Some people deal with their feelings in a superficial way. They know that there are feelings involved with their behavior, but they don't think that these feelings drive their behavior. Consider the following 2 people:

KEN

Ken fancied himself to be a ladies man. He had a fairly regular pattern. He pursued each woman who attracted him, told her that she was the "one," slept with her a few times and then broke up with her.

Ken kept track of the number of women he had slept with. If his stories are to be believed, that count was in the hundreds. Ken saw all of this as a thrilling game. Any hurt that he experienced or caused was written off as part of the game. He said, "Everyone knows that this is a game. There are times when someone's going to get their feelings hurt. That's just the way it goes. If they can't handle that, they shouldn't play the game."

Ken thought he had everything under control. He enjoyed the chase and the conquest. All of his moves were predictable. He kept his feelings in check and "never allowed himself to get too involved with any one woman." When he started to have deeper feelings for a woman, he quickly pursued another woman. When a woman told Ken that she was not happy or that she was hurting about something, Ken told her not to be so sensitive. He told her that he was a "free spirit who couldn't be tied down." If she rejected that idea, Ken rejected her.

Some of Ken's friends envied his life and his lifestyle. It seemed so carefree and exciting. That was true as long as you didn't look too closely. Small issues started to arise for Ken.

For the first time in his life, Ken had not been able to achieve or maintain an erection. This typically occurred after he slept with a woman a few times. Ken wrote this off as "just being bored with the same woman." Ken's sleep patterns became disturbed when he was not dating anyone. He often woke up in the middle of the night, unable to return to sleep. Ken's quick answer was that he "needed sex to get a good night's sleep." Ken rarely spent much time alone because "it is boring to be by him." He usually spent 4-5 nights a week in bars during these periods. His drinking increased when he was alone.

When I asked Ken about his picture of himself as a man, he quickly talked about his sexual prowess and his ability to "go all night long." When I asked him about feeling lonely, he responded by saying that "lonely is for losers." When I asked him, how he thought women felt about him, he said, "They should feel lucky that I want to be with them." Rarely, if ever did Ken acknowledge his feelings of hurt or the feelings of hurt that he caused for his partners. Why? Ken's view of how a man behaved was that "you loved 'em and then left 'em." He wasn't going to get trapped into marrying someone. A quick glance at his philandering dad, Bud, explained much of Ken's behavior. Bud left Ken's mom when Ken was only 6. He never remarried and died alone. Ken seemed destined to live out the script that Bud had written.

For Ken and others like him, he stays in his head and avoids dealing with his feelings most of the time. He has a quick answer for everything. He is quick to tell a joke, brag about himself and his track record. There is rarely a quiet moment when you sit with Ken. Getting "too deep or too heavy" doesn't work for Ken. He wants to keep it light all of the time. Ken claims that he doesn't have time or interest to deal with the hurt he feels or the hurt he causes. Unwittingly and unfortunately, it just continues to control his life.

EDITH

This is not just true for men. Edith was 37 years old. She was an exceptionally well dressed, executive with a large national retailer. She was up on all of the latest fashions and trends. If you wanted to know what was "trending" at the moment, Edith could tell you. Edith was on line all of the time. Edith thought of herself as "on the cutting edge." A true trend setter. A hard look at her script suggests something a bit different.

Edith's mother, Bernadette, was a tenured professor of English at a private university. She was at the top of her field, but there was a policy that faculty could no longer teach after age 70. Despite her stellar credentials and career, Bernadette was forced into retirement. Removed from the environment that she had loved for over 30 years, Bernadette quickly became depressed, became afflicted with pancreatic cancer and died within 2 years. Edith's father, Mark, had a similar story. He was a two-star admiral in the Coast Guard. The upper echelon of the Coast Guard is quite small and Mark was eventually passed over for further promotion. He was retired with great pomp and circumstance. However, being unprepared for retirement, he floundered and quickly found himself depressed, unhappy and alone after Bernadette died.

Observing the fate of her parents, Edith is determined to be vigilant about her own career. She wants to be up-to-date on everything in her world. She is always reading about the latest and greatest. If Edith was thrilled to do this and received great enjoyment from doing it, there would be no issue. The issue is that Edith feels compelled to do this. She can't tell you why she does it. She just does it. When I asked her why she is so driven, she said: "It's a young person's world nowadays. I can't afford to let it pass me by." Fear is a great motivator. It can drive you to great heights. BUT, it can also control your behavior. As Edith gets older, this compulsion could have even greater impact on the way she lives her life.

AVOIDING OR POSTPONING DEALING WITH YOUR FEELINGS

When traumatic events occur suddenly, your body and mind goes into shock and you simply react to the situation at hand. There is little or no time to deal with how you feel. You do what you have to do until the event is over. Once you have navigated through the shock phase, however, you can choose to work through your feelings and "reframe" them. Hopefully you'll work through them fully so that you can come out on the other side of a traumatic situation still able to live your life on your terms.

JOE

In 1978. a Pacific Southwest Airlines plane collided with a small private plane over San Diego. The airliner with over 100 passengers on board crashed a few miles from the airport. I was an adjunct psychology professor at a local graduate school at the time. One of my M.A. students happened to be one of the first responders at the scene. Joe was a Viet Nam war veteran who had seen his share of bloodshed and suffering. He was one of the first responders at the site and went to work in a professional manner.

During a class session later that week, Joe revealed to the class that he had been involved in the clean-up at the site. Despite his war experience, he reported that "he had never seen such carnage in his life. There were body parts everywhere. The heat level was asphyxiating, because the crash had occurred at a time when Santa Ana winds were blowing in from the desert outside of San Diego." Since this was a graduate psychology class, one classmate asked, "What were you thinking about as you were performing your duties?" The first responder answered in candor when he replied, "I just wanted to do my job and make sure I didn't throw up in front of my men." That seemed to satisfy the questioner and nothing more was said about the situation during that class session.

Two weeks later, Joe called me up and asked if he could meet with me prior to our class session. When we met in private, he quietly confided, "Doc, every time I drive by the scene on the freeway, I hear voices screaming. I am having dreams of people crying out for help and I can't do anything to help them. Am I going crazy?"

I reassured Joe that everything he was hearing and dreaming about was perfectly normal and entirely predictable given what he had experienced. His response team had been told that they might experience visual or auditory hallucinations in the weeks following the crash. However, at no point, were they were not encouraged to talk about their feelings openly. No time or opportunity was set aside during work hours to deal with what they had experienced. Each of them had been given a contact number for a local EAP (Employee Assistance Program) to use if they felt the need. Most of the men did not avail themselves of this resource, because "they were men's men and they thought they could handle it."

I asked Joe a few simple questions designed to help him process the trauma he had experienced. I also wanted to help him unearth any other feelings that might be affecting his response to the trauma.

1) How did you feel while you were completing your work?
2) How did you feel after the site was cleaned up?
3) What else could you have done at the site?
4) Since there were no survivors, was there anything else you could have done to help the victims or their families?
5) Did you do your best when you were working at the scene?
6) What other thoughts and feelings have occurred to you since the event?

After asking each question, I just sat and listened. I offered few responses. I repeated back the significant comments he had made and reflected back the feelings I was picking up from him. I offered empathy for how difficult it must have been to have arrived at the site to find no survivors, just body parts.

I suggested to him that he might want to tell and retell the story several times to people that he trusted. Each time he might find that he could get in touch with other feelings that lay beneath the surface. I assured him that in time, he would be able to accept that he had done all that he could at the site. He might also realize the life is fragile and that there is much to be thankful for, despite the tragedies that randomly occur. As the class progressed, Joe reported feeling better and being more at peace with himself. He was also able to reach out to other first responders and offer them a sympathetic ear. Although he needed more work to process his feelings of hurt, Joe was on the right path towards rising up from his hurt.

Compare Joe's progression through his hurt with that of Lenny. Unfortunately, Lenny's case did not have the same kind of positive resolution.

LENNY

I knew a veteran, Lenny, who experienced a traumatic set of assaults and confrontations during basic training in the Army during the late 1960's. Lenny was Jewish and was sent to complete his basic training at a military base in Texas, where the officers had not had a lot of contact with Jewish people before. There he experienced a frightening and constant series of attacks and derogatory harangues. His life was repeatedly threatened by a sergeant and a small cadre of his fellow soldiers. Despite performing in a stellar fashion he was told that "no Jew was ever gonna outshine others in this outfit."

His attempts to complain about this abusive treatment were met with scoffing and derision by the lieutenant and the captain who oversaw the unit. Lenny received undue work assignments that involved cleaning toilets, cleaning floors with tooth brushes and carrying extremely heavy equipment. He completed all of these assignments without complaint and accepted that this was just part of being in the Army.

After several months of this abusive treatment, Lenny was transferred to another base. At that point, the nightmares started to occur. Loud unexpected noises resulted in his becoming startled and increasingly hyper-vigilant His sleep patterns were no longer reasonable and he could no longer sleep for more than a few hours each evening. In restaurants and in other large rooms, he always preferred to sit in the corner where he could see the front door and survey all that was happening in the room. He started to shy away from large crowds where he felt that he was in the midst of a sea of people.

His entire trauma occurred during the 1960's. The diagnosis of PTSD (Post Traumatic Stress Disorder) was not in common usage at that time. The nightmares continued, but Lenny was able to keep his life together, working as a substitute teacher in a rural school district until the 1980's when one event triggered his concern.

Upon discharge from the service, he quietly moved into a small home in the mountains hidden away from others. He had few trusted friends and purchased several rifles that were easily accessible in his home.

People that knew Lenny just wrote off most of his behavior as "unusual or eccentric." Other than these peculiarities, he seemed to be a friendly, positive individual.

One day at school, a teenage boy came up behind Lenny and playfully put his arms around him from behind. Lenny became startled and without thinking quickly flipped the boy over his shoulder to the ground. Within a few seconds, Lenny's heart began beating very rapidly and that he was covered in sweat. These feelings continued as he explained what happened to the principal of the school. Lenny was asked to leave the school and never taught another student after that.

Lenny was encouraged by other veterans he had met at the VA to at least read articles about PTSD. He started to attend a PTSD group with other veterans. He quickly established a relationship with a PTSD counselor, where he uncovered a significant issue. Lenny could not reconcile the fact that he absorbed all of the discrimination, abusive treatment and harangues from his sergeant, without ever once striking back. For years, Lenny had maintained a deeply hidden belief. He felt that: "I should have killed that guy. That's what any man worth his salt would have done. Left him for dead. He would have gotten what he deserved."

Lenny had been greatly influenced by his father, Brett, who had risen to a high level in the corporate world. Brett had been successful in many of his ventures and was known as a "man who didn't take crap from anyone." Brett rarely felt out of control in his world. Trying to live up to the image of a man that his father had projected for him, Lenny had volunteered to go to the Army in order to become a man.

When he looked back on his Army experience, Lenny felt that he had reacted in an "impotent" way. This reaction weighed heavily and constantly on Lenny's mind, since the time of the assaults. How could he be a real man, when he had reacted so poorly? Surely, other men would have confronted the situation in a more aggressive manner. The bottom line was that Lenny, "the adult," could not forgive Lenny, "the boy," for not reacting in a more "manly" fashion.

Lenny remained stuck at this point. The nightmares continued several times a week and his startle reflex was as strong as ever. The irony was that Lenny claimed to understand the issue. He understood the logic of his father's influence on his decisions. He also understood his inability to forgive himself. He was just unwilling to do much about it. For him, feeling hurt meant that he was weak, and he refused to be weak. In his mind, it was better not to feel the hurt at all. Unless, he was willing to process all of the aspects of his hurt more completely, he would never be healed.

Understanding your feelings and processing your feelings are two entirely different activities. Whenever you apply logic to a largely emotional situation, you are not fully processing all that is going on.

Understanding the issue typically accounts for 10% of the battle. Deciding to deal with the issue accounts for the next 30%. Doing something about it and rising up from the hurt is the last and hardest 60%. These are not hard and fast numbers.

For some people, the emotional blockage is so strong that they can't understand or even imagine what is beneath the surface. For them, first steps will be much more challenging. For other people, there is the possibility that growth through the process will not be linear. They may achieve insights simultaneously to making decisions that allow them to move into action more quickly. For Lenny, the tragedy was that Lenny went to his grave, never able to forgive the young boy who did not stand up for himself.

Many men and women grew up with role models that either never acknowledged hurt or shrugged it off with apparent disdain. Do you know people like this? Are you one of them?

While it is hard to face long repressed feelings of hurt, the consequences of not doing so are significant. In summary, it comes down to how you want to handle the pain. It can be handled directly or it can stay with you for the rest of your life.

DEALING WITH DEEP FEELINGS

While it isn't easy or always pleasant to deal with deep feelings of hurt. Sometimes, those feelings emerge at unexpected times. Sometimes they are triggered by seemingly disconnected bits of conversation. However, once those feelings reach the surface, it provides you with an opportunity to rise up from your hurt.

NICOLE

Nicole was a 29-year-old woman who was employed as an emergency room nurse at a local hospital. She was unmarried and had not had many long term relationships with men. She worked hard and was now enrolled in a BA program in psychology. She was a diligent student in a class that I was teaching, completed all of her work and often spoke up with pertinent questions and opinions. The class was comparatively small, having only 16 students.

Near the end of one of our class sessions, another student commented on the rose bushes that had been recently planted in the rear of the building. She commented on how pretty it looked to see roses of every color: red, orange, white, even yellow. As soon as she said the color "yellow," Nicole's face turned ashen. It was as if she had seen a ghost. Within moments, she was tearfully collecting her books and racing out of the classroom. Other students' efforts to stop her were unsuccessful. She was gone.

Her abrupt departure raised a red flag in my mind. I waited two days and then called her at her home. I asked her how she was doing. She said that she had not been able to go to work since the class. She had spent the last 2 days alone at her home overwhelmed by many different emotions. She said that she seemed to alternate between crying, becoming furious, being frightened, being confused and feeling like she was totally out of control. She worried that she was losing her mind. I asked her, if she had any idea as to what was causing this outpouring of deep feelings. She said she didn't. She asked my opinion and I said that if she was still experiencing these feelings, she could come to my office the next day and I would try to help her get to the bottom of the issue. She agreed.

When I called Nicole the next day, she was still sobbing on the phone. I asked if she thought that she could make it to campus. She agreed. Shortly after she arrived, I started asking her several questions:

1) Did she like roses?
2) Had she received roses from anyone in her life?
3) Did she associate roses with special events? Weddings? Confirmations? Funerals?

4) What did the color yellow represent to her?
5) Did she remember the song "Tie a Yellow Ribbon Around the Old Oak Tree?"

None of these questions triggered any emotional response. I then asked if she remembered any yellow roses near her house when she was growing up. Her eyes opened wide as the tears rapidly flowed down her cheek. She said, "Oh, my God, I know what this is about." As she reached for tissues to wipe her eyes, I suggested that tissues would only stop her from feeling. I asked her to report what she had just remembered.

She began to describe a scene that she had long since repressed/blocked/ purged from her consciousness. She described walking to school when she was 7 years old down a different block that she never had been on before. There was a hedge and some yellow roses planted by an old house. As she bent over to smell the roses, a man grabbed her and started to pull her behind the hedge. He groped her and began to remove his pants. He told Nicole not to scream or he would kill her. Nicole didn't know what to do. Luckily, as he was pulling down his pants, he fell over. Nicole took the chance to run away as fast as she could. She never went down that block again and never told anyone about the incident.

Suddenly, all of her feelings made sense. Sadness. Anger. Confusion. Powerlessness. The initial outpouring of these feelings was cathartic, but it was not the end of processing her feelings. She began to see a female therapist who helped her relive the experience and feel all the different feelings that she had. Since Nicole had been too afraid to tell anyone about the event, she also encountered feelings of shame, distrust and revulsion. In the long run she had to deal with her fear of not reporting the event to her parents or anyone else at school. She felt stupid. She felt like that man probably assaulted other kids in her community as well and that she had done nothing to stop him.

It took a while for Nicole to accept and forgive herself. After all, she was only seven. Nothing had prepared her for what to do and how to respond to such a horrific attack. In less than two months, Nicole was feeling much better. She even planted roses in her front yard. Red roses. She was not yet ready for yellow.

Once the floodgates opened up for Nicole, many feelings emerged. The same is true for the rest of us. There isn't one correct method or order to deal with the feelings. Some of the feelings will have to re-experienced and relived several times before they can be reframed. It can feel like you are losing your mind.

CHARLENE

Some people get stuck in just one feeling. Every time Charlene gets sad, she gives herself 2 days to feel sorry. She calls it her "pity party." She stays away from other people. She cries and then asks herself what the tears are for. She doesn't see joy in the world. She gives herself permission to be sad. To sob. To feel empty. To feel as if she doesn't have a friend in the world. All of this works for her. By the 3rd day, Charlene gets angry at herself for her self-indulgence and then begins a ritual designed to move her out of the house and in a new direction. It may not work for you. It just works for Charlene.

Some people lie in bed and fall asleep instantly. Some people can't sleep at all. Some people eat everything there is in the house. Others are sick to their stomach. What you will feel will be unique to you. The important thing is to experience what you feel and to spend whatever time you can allowing old thoughts and scripts to come into your consciousness. Once that occurs, you can begin to accept the feelings, forgive yourself for any actions that you regret, and start to "reframe" your hurt.

BARRY

Barry was a big fan of "encounter groups" that were popular many years ago. In those groups, individuals would gather and talk about how they were feeling in the "here and now." Barry was a veteran of these groups having participated in many of them. He had shared many difficult events in his own life, his struggles with his own sexuality, and the horror he felt as a fire burned down his house when he was a youngster. The rest of the group was also composed of people who were willing to explore their deeper feelings. Barry was attending one session without anything on his mind to share when he listened to the story of another participant, Fred.

Fred began to tell a story about how he had dealt with the death of his mother. It had been almost five years to the day that his mother had died. He had just been to the cemetery to visit her grave prior to the session. Fred had been living in San Francisco at the time. He poignantly described how his mother had taken ill very suddenly and had quickly gone into a coma in a local New York hospital.

His father had called him and told him to fly to NYC on the first flight that he could get. Fred frantically went to the airport the next day and flew across the country only to find that his mother had died during that morning, while he was on the plane. He softly said, "I never had a chance to say goodbye."

When Barry heard that, a flood of tears gushed as he started to sob uncontrollably. The session leader asked Fred if it was OK to refocus the group's attention and check in with Barry. Barry had flashed on an incident in his own life which was almost identical.

Barry had been hitchhiking in Europe with a friend of his, Howie, during the summer. They had been to several countries in a short time span and Barry was feeling a bit under the weather. He decided to stay at the youth hostel, while Howie went out to explore the countryside. Tragically, as Howie was standing by the side of the road, a speeding motorist came around a corner too quickly, didn't see Howie and crushed him against a tree. Howie died instantly.

As soon as Barry was notified, he accompanied the body of his friend back to the USA. Howie was buried shortly thereafter in a small ceremony only attended by Howie's family.

Barry began to scream, "I never got a chance to say goodbye either." The night before we were laughing and having a beer and 2 days later I am on a plane taking his body back home. I never told Howie how I felt about him. I never thought that I wouldn't see him again. It just never occurred to me." Barry had been in shock when he got the news and made the arrangements for the transport of Howie's body.

Since he didn't attend the funeral, he didn't have a chance to talk to Howie's family and tell them how sorry he was. Barry knew it wasn't his fault that Howie had died, but there was just so much he wanted to say about Howie. So many memories that came flooding back. During that session, Barry was asked to say what he wanted to say to Howie. Words and tears flowed for half an hour. Shortly after, Barry collapsed in a heap He was spent.

Feelings aren't typically fully processed in one setting. Crying tears and speaking from the heart are part of the process. But remember that not all of the memories arise at one time. There were many other encounter group sessions where Barry would ask to speak to Howie again. There were sessions at the cemetery where Barry would go alone to chat with Howie. Death and other major hurts take time before people are ready to move on.

The impact of this event was not just for Barry. I was one of the participants in that group and on that night I swore to myself that I would never leave anyone I cared for deeply without telling them how I felt. When I call my daughter and other dear friends, I usually end each call reminding them of how much I love them and how much they mean to me. I may die suddenly at some point, but I won't die feeling like I didn't get a chance to express my own deep feelings.

For Barry, the encounter group provided him with an opportunity to process his feelings deeply and to move on. You must find the right time, the right place and the right situation to help you process your feelings. Then you can move on as well.

HOW TO PROCESS YOUR FEELINGS

At the primary level the answer is simple. Feel your feelings. Allow them to wash over you when you have the time and privacy to do so. Think about where those feelings come from. Think about old scripts that may be attached to them. Scripts are decisions that you once made which may have been entirely appropriate and helpful at the time that you made them. However, you may have forgotten about these decisions and are not aware of their impact upon your current behavior.

That said, there is no single correct way to feel those feelings.

When you feel hurt by events, you may react with the fight-flight response. You may feel angry or frightened. There is nothing wrong with this first reaction. The issue is what you do with that feeling. You have a variety of options:

1) You may find it so uncomfortable, that you attempt to distract yourself to avoid the feeling. The alcohol, medication, cigarettes,

food or whatever you turn to may serve you well for that moment. However, the next day brings you right back to the same feelings. Unless you constantly distract yourself, you will not be feeling better than before you distracted yourself the first time. You may even feel WORSE when you realize the self-defeating nature of your cycle.

2) You may use a variety of psychological defense mechanisms (which are largely unconscious) to keep those feelings in check. You could rationalize what happened and assume the victim stance, where you feel that others took advantage of you. You could intellectualize the feelings and find a "logical" reason to explain what happened, thus consciously relieving you of responsibility for your feelings.

3) You could react quickly to the event/other person with a fit of rage, telling them off in no uncertain terms. On the surface, this seems like you are dealing with how you feel. However, since the rage can be out of proportion with the triggering event, it may suggest that the rage has more to do with something deeper than just the incident at hand.

4) You may simply try to forget about how you feel. You may think that dwelling on your feelings will only make it worse. Men who have the "stiff upper lip syndrome" pride themselves on showing little or no emotion. The idea is that "real men" don't allow themselves to be hurt. The truth is that holding everything in more often results in sickness and death at an earlier age. Real men shouldn't have to end up sick or dead.

OR YOU CAN CHOOSE A MORE PRODUCTIVE LONG RUN STRATEGY:

5) You can immerse yourself in your feelings, feel them deeply and see what emerges from your mind. In this manner, you can understand your current feeling and potentially the script that accompanies these feelings.

Consider the following example. When I make presentations about uncovering old scripts, I often ask the women in the audience if they have a strong need to immediately sort and put all of their clothes away when they return home from work. While there are men who feel the same need, I have found that it is more prevalent with women. This behavior seems to be a prudent way to keep the home neat and to preserve the value and appearance of their clothes. Most of the women in the audience usually agree that they do this regularly. However, there is a BIG difference between doing it because you choose to do it and feeling compelled to do it. There are always a few women who MUST do this regardless of the time they get home, how they feel or what condition they are in.

I ask them to try the following exercise. I suggest that when they have a three day weekend and the kids are not around, that they should try a different approach to dealing with their clothes. Instead of the usual sorting into piles of whites, darks and dry cleaning, I ask them to do something else. I ask them to stand in a room of the house that is private (the bedroom is a good room to use), draw the curtains and take their clothes off while standing in the middle of the room. I ask them to then hurl the clothes in different directions in the room and LEAVE THE CLOTHES wherever they land for the next 72 hours. That means that a blouse could end up on the bedpost, while a bra could end up dangling from a curtain rod. Then I ask them to put on other clothes (the exercise has nothing to do with nudity) and sit in the room periodically over the next 3 days. I urge them to resist the temptation to put the clothes away until 72 hours have passed.

Most of the women who feel compelled to put their clothes away start to laugh nervously when they hear about the exercise or immediately start to shake their heads and say: "No Way." The very thought of the exercise conjures up a frightening feeling for them. I plead with them to at least try it once and we begin to discuss what will happen.

I ask them what they think they will learn during the first 24 hours. Most of the women say, "I will learn that the world won't end if I don't immediately put my clothes away every day." I suggest to them that it will take quite a bit longer to believe that idea, because they have not yet discovered the script and the emotions that are driving their behavior. I suggest instead that for the first 24 hours, they will probably just think angry thoughts about me or about how stupid the exercise is. They will feel that it is a waste of time and will feel like they want to put all of the clothes away at that exact moment.

In the second 24-hour period, the real learning may begin to occur. If the woman spends time in the room with the clothes strewn all over the furniture, she may begin to get into contact with the script that is driving her behavior. Most young girls were told by their mother that, "good girls hang up their clothes." Girls at the impressionable age of 6 really want to be "good girls" and want to continue to receive favorable attention from their mother.

When you were six years old, this was a great script for you and for your mother. The script made your clothes look nicer and last longer. It resulted in one less task for mom to do as well. It was probably a good way to get you to learn how to deal with your clothes. It continues to be a good behavior today, still protecting and prolonging the value of your clothes.

The issue only becomes problematic when it is no longer your choice. The same behavior can now become a compulsion, which must be completed regardless of the time of day and condition that you are in. The worst part of it is that, if you don't hang up the clothes, you start to feel uncomfortable until you do it. You may want to reconsider the old script and ask yourself: "Do I have to do it every single time? At 45 years old, being a good girl may mean something completely different."

Is it time for you to get in touch with your old scripts and CHOOSE which ones to keep and which ones to discard?

This is the critical issue when dealing with emotions. Many of your emotional reactions are rooted in the past. They are driven by the way you and others in your environment reacted to other events. Those emotions may have had a lot to do with what you were told and how you were expected to behave.

Once you can recall the original scripts from your childhood, you can now evaluate them again and CHOOSE whether or not to continue to let them drive your current behavior. Becoming aware of those scripts and reconsidering their present value is one of the crucial elements in "reframing" how you feel. In the long run, it is one of the more important factors that allow you to rise up from your hurt.

Your emotions can easily become entangled when you are hurting. Emotions become intertwined. One of the common examples is the relationship between anger and hurt. You often feel anger externally, while you hurt internally.

You may have a script that allows you to only be comfortable with one of those feelings. Therefore, instead of getting angry in a situation, you may only feel hurt. Conversely, instead of dealing with feelings of hurt, you may only lash out at others, blaming them for your feelings.

Sadness, depression, apathy and confusion can also become intertwined. The key idea is to do the best that you can to separate these feelings. Each may be quite significant on its own. Each feeling can be related to a separate script. No book can fully catalogue all of your emotions.

You are unique as are all of your life experiences. Therefore, just allow yourself to feel what you feel. If you can embark on this process, you may find ways to "reframe" and rise up from your hurt.

CAREFRONTATION

Carefrontation is a process you can use after you have allowed yourself to get in touch with your deep feelings. Hopefully, you will be able to remember some of the scripts that you created early in your life that add intensity to your feelings today. Carefronting your feelings involves a combination of acceptance and forgiveness.

When you were younger, you reacted to situations in the best way that you knew at that time. As a child, dealing with parents, teachers and even friends, you often accepted what you were told as being valid and true. You may have absorbed scripts because you were told to or because they seemed right at the time. Maybe you didn't feel like you had any real choices. Some of the scripts may have been forced upon you by the situation. Perhaps you didn't have a standard by which to judge whether or not those scripts were good for you.

At this point, it doesn't really matter why you accepted those scripts. *What matters today is that they are still active in determining your behaviors today.* Accepting that fact and forgiving yourself for some of your unusual or bad choices can be of great benefit to you.

Yesterday is the only part of your life that you can't do anything about. Your real choices involve what you will do today, tomorrow and for the rest of your life. Here are examples of how several other people have chosen to "reframe" their scripts.

MARVIN

"When I was younger, I was bigger than most of the other kids my age. I looked older too. I probably acted like a bully at times, although I didn't really mean to harm anyone. That was just the best way I knew to have fun. I did many things then that I would do differently today. When I look back at the situation, I have regrets. I could choose to dwell on those regrets and vow to never do those things again. Instead, I now understand that I am a human being who is not perfect. Whatever mistakes I made, I am responsible for my own behaviors. I own what I did, AND I will use that power to choose to behave differently from now on."

JASON

"I had a dad who never thought I would amount to anything. He made fun of me all the time. He never once told me he was proud of me. The only way that I could feel good about myself was to hang out with my friends and do stupid things to make them laugh. I was always the class clown and never believed that I could do well in school. I always felt that I was going to end up in the same kind of dead end job that my dad had, working in a factory. I just got by. I was a cutup and never really applied myself seriously to anything. Sometimes, I feel sad because I wasted so much time not even trying to improve my situation. Now I am going back to school to get my AA degree. I even think I can complete a 4-year degree. When I start to feel like I'm not good enough, I go to the cemetery where my dad is buried and tell the headstone that I am going to make it."

WILMA

"When I was a teenager, I ran around and slept around a lot. I always had dates and thought that I was very popular. I never realized that everyone at school thought of me as the town slut. I thought I was popular with boys because I looked pretty, wore pretty clothes and laughed at a lot of their stupid jokes. I guess I should have realized that something was wrong. I never ended up in any long-term relationships. I would see a boy for a few months and then that would be that. After I started going to church again in my twenties, I thought I was going to hell for what I had done. I stayed alone quite a bit, afraid to date again. I thought all boys just wanted sex from girls. Nothing else. Now I have a good job and am beginning to feel like I can be proud of something other than how I look. I go slowly with men now, so that I can see if they really like me. I don't think I am going to hell. I think God gives us chances to turn our lives around."

JANET

"I grew up in a very poor family. We just got by. I never had any new clothes. I always had to wear hand me downs from my sister. I hated that. All of the kids at school made fun of me when school started in September each year. They all had new clothes, but I never had any. My family went to the local thrift store to get clothes, and I just felt awful. I felt it wasn't fair that I never had new shoes. I met a wonderful guy and we got married recently. Although we are not rich, I can now afford to go shopping every month. I am always buying something new. Even when I don't need anything, I still buy stuff. I am just figuring out that I am making up for the clothes I didn't have as a kid. I am slowly learning that clothes don't determine what kind of person you are. Whether or not you have new clothes doesn't make you a better or worse person. I am now thinking about what else I can do in the world and what really matters to me."

Everyone's story is unique and different. I am sure that your story is different from the ones that you have read. Hopefully you were buoyed by the fact that each of these people CHOSE to let go of parts of their past and see a different, more vibrant tomorrow. That is what you can do as well.

If you want to rise up from your hurt, you must be able to offer yourself empathy, understanding and support. Whatever you have done is in the past. Today you have a new opportunity to reconsider all of your scripts and determine which ones still work for you and which ones require modification or deletion. It is time to determine who you want to be and move in that direction.

There are payoffs or psychological benefits for continuing to judge your behaviors too harshly (such as taking the victim stance and not having to make further changes.) But those payoffs pale in comparison to being able to free yourself from your past. You will learn more in the coming chapters about how to discover and understand your payoffs for your behaviors.

Life is too short not to forgive yourself many times over for missteps and false starts. Although you probably make several errors every day, remember that you also have the ability to forgive yourself several times a day and move on. Rising up from your hurt is about getting on with the rest of your life in a happier way.

Chapter 4

HOW YOUR BRAIN DEALS WITH HURT

As a psychologist, therapist, life coach and student of human behavior for over forty years, I have listed a few assumptions that I strongly believe in when I view people dealing with their hurt. In order to help you deal with your hurt, I want YOU to consider how these assumptions may apply to YOU. These assumptions include:

1. Preserving your self-concept.
2. Avoiding pain and finding pleasure.
3. Understanding payoffs for your behavior.
4. Wanting your surroundings to be orderly and structured, consistent, reliable, and coherent.
5. Avoiding cognitive dissonance.
6. Knowing the difference between emotion and logic.
7) Understanding intention and impact.

1) SELF CONCEPT

Humans seek to preserve our SELF CONCEPT at all costs. Rule #1 is preserving your "SELF CONCEPT." Rule #2 is remembering Rule #1.

"SELF CONCEPT" is the picture you have created in your mind of yourself and the meaning that you have attributed to your existence. It can include your values and mission as well as an answer to the eternal life question: "What is your purpose and goal for being on this planet at this time?"

It usually is an integration of many factors:

a. how everyone around you treated you as you grew up
b. what others expected from you
c. what you expected from yourself
d. who you were told to be by everyone around you
e. who you decided to emulate
f. who you decided to become
g. what you experienced in the media
h. what your life experiences have been
i. what you have wished, dreamed and fantasized about.

There are a myriad of other factors that may have affected your self-concept as well. There is no universal formula that each person uses. Therefore, with or without intention, you have created a SELF CONCEPT of yourself, which you constantly seek to live up to. You may even think of it as being true to yourself.

SELF CONCEPTS can lead people to behave in a wide variety of ways. You may be sustaining your SELF CONCEPT at great personal cost and pain. For some people just staying physically alive at all costs seems to be preeminent. For others, the sustenance of their family is paramount. Religious fanatics have proclaimed that faith in their deity outweighs all other earthly considerations. Gang members will lay their lives on the line for their brethren when they feel that their colors have been disrespected.

For a soldier, smothering a grenade in a fox hole with his own body to save his fellow soldier may be the only honorable course of action. Another soldier may refuse to leave an injured comrade on the battlefield, choosing instead to carry him out at great personal risk. A suicide bomber who blows himself up in a crowded "infidel" marketplace sees himself as pleasing his G-d and eagerly awaits his celestial reward.

All of these people are simply seeking to live up to the picture they have created of themselves. Can you describe your SELF CONCEPT? Who are you at your core? What do you strive to become? How do you define yourself (without just listing your job or your hobbies?) What is most critical to YOUR SELF CONCEPT? What must you have in order for you to feel good about yourself and to be true to yourself?

Your answer is probably a product of your genetics, your environment, your culture, your parents, your education, your experiences and the media you were exposed to among many other factors.

Ultimately, you make choices that fulfill your SELF CONCEPT. These choices may not be right for anyone else, but you deem them correct for yourself. Is your current SELF CONCEPT driven by an old script from the past that was written a long time ago?

The critical issue is that your SELF CONCEPT is integrally involved with how you deal with your hurt. For instance, Lenny (from Chapter 3) very much wanted to live up to his father's image of a man. He wanted to feel that he was in control of everything that happened to him. He simply could not forgive his actions as a boy when faced with discrimination in the army. He buried his feelings and instead accepted his PTSD symptoms and nightmares as the price he had to pay for his actions.

Is it possible that you are accepting hurt in your life in order to maintain your SELF CONCEPT? Is it worth it? Is your SELF CONCEPT driven by an old script from the past or by conscious choices that you have made more recently? Old scripts may have made sense at the original time you created them. If you don't periodically reconsider their worth and reality-test them occasionally, you may find that they have outlived their utility. Would you rather have your SELF CONCEPT AND your current level of hurt or are you open to changing your SELF CONCEPT and experiencing more happiness?

How you choose to deal with your hurt will fit with your sense of "who you are" and your SELF CONCEPT.

YOU are more than your job, your hobbies, your roles and responsibilities. Before moving forward, ask and answer this question first: WHO ARE YOU?

2) PAIN AVOIDANCE and PLEASURE ACQUISITION

How you deal with the pain/pleasure ratio strongly influences your behavior and choices when you are faced with problems. Neurochemistry (particularly levels of dopamine), genetics and early learning experiences determine the initial relative strengths of pleasure vs. pain in your motivational set. Learning, experience and perceived deprivations continue to exert influence as you grow older.

The pleasure/pain ratio is not a constant that you can attain. There is no set homeostatic level that is ideal for you all of the time. It varies throughout your lifetime. Simplistically, I could suggest that you always want to maximize pleasure and minimize pain. However, that does not accurately describe reality at all times. Sometimes, a little pain now and then (e.g., a flu shot, a shot of a dental anesthetic like Novocaine, pushing one's physical limits in the gym, staying late at the office to complete an unpleasant task or just having a good cry) can pave the way for greater pleasure in the future.

Some people go further in one direction. One extreme fitness group defines pain as weakness leaving your body. Pain (at least in tolerable amounts) is viewed as the first step to real growth. In their view, we don't begin to grow in our physical stamina until we have faced and overcome our pain.

The other direction can be problematic as well. Constant joy, pleasure and ecstasy, although seemingly desirable, can lose their attractiveness over time. Imagine eating only your favorite food day after day. After a while, it might be less satisfying. People who work in ice cream or pizza parlors eventually lose their taste for those foods. Long-term employees at the Hershey's Chocolate Factory in Pennsylvania, though allowed to eat as much chocolate as they like while on the job, eventually choose not to do so.

Experiencing both pain and pleasure provides a strong framework for understanding what truly makes you happy and sad. You can never truly know pleasure or pain without experiencing both of them and having a context by which to compare them.

What is clear is that you are forever doing a balancing act between pleasure and pain. Life becomes a never ending cost-benefit analysis, a risk-reward conundrum where the most desirable option is not a constant; instead, it is an equilibrium point. The irony is that once that point is reached, it must be constantly readjusted. It is almost impossible to stay at any equilibrium point. Life becomes a constant process of fine tuning.

Past memories of hurt are more easily recalled than memories of pleasure due to their relevance to preserving your SELF CONCEPT.

While random rewards can truly be thrilling, random punishments or embarrassments can truly be debilitating. Our brains seem to be hard wired to remember past hurts, disappointments, embarrassments and trauma more so than past successes, pleasures and accolades. This becomes quite important when people deal with their problems.

When you remember the hurt from previous encounters with an issue, you tend to shy away from wanting to deal with it again. Pain avoidance seems a far better option, on the surface, than another immediate encounter or experience with potential fear or failure, even if it might potentially lead to greater happiness in the future.

You may quickly, consciously or unconsciously, decide that the current amount of discomfort that you are feeling when dealing with a current issue is much more palatable than the possible larger amount of discomfort associated with other potential options to deal with your issues differently. Since you have already accepted and "gotten used to your current level of pain," you define it as tolerable. It is known. It hasn't killed you so far. On the surface, it doesn't seem to be getting that much worse.

Staying at that level of pain, you can easily lose perspective as to how painful it really is. People around you can often see the level of pain associated with the problem more clearly than you can because they have not become acclimated to it. They have not accepted that level of pain as "normal."

Additionally, some people adopt a sophisticated psychological defense mechanism in which they convince themselves that the potential pain associated with "digging into their psyches" will become so unbearable that they will never be able to emerge from that pain. They fear that they will become lost in the pain forever. While that can happen, the probability of such a reaction is quite low. Nonetheless, this defense mechanism provides a high entry barrier to dealing with current pain.

A few words about psychological defenses may help you understand this a bit better. Psychological defenses have 2 main characteristics. First, they are unconscious, so you may not be aware that you are even using them. Second, they are brought into play as a function of "your perception of being under attack." That is the reason that they are referred to as defense or self-protection mechanisms. The irony in this case is that people perceive self-inquiry into past issues as a potentially harmful attack, rather than as an attempt to reduce pain and bring about more happiness in the long run. The defense, therefore, serves to keep the person in current pain, rather than protect them from future pain. If you feel this way, you may need reassurance and support from others to help you stay on track.

For some people, staying "stuck in pain" can amount to "mental suicide by butter knife." It takes a long time, and you will experience constant low levels of pain as your emotional lifeblood trickles out. Strong short-term pain memories overwhelm potential long-term possibilities of pleasure. When you are on the brink of an uncertain event, a subconscious search is conducted to determine past associations and experiences with pain and pleasure outcomes. You compare and evaluate the past in terms of attempts vs. outcomes. At a sub-cortical level, you quickly form an inclination towards the Go vs. No Go decision before you are aware of any real thinking about it. That becomes the basis for your intuitive feelings about the problem.

Malcolm Gladwell in "Blink" referred to this as "thin slicing." He suggested that thin slicing was often as accurate in decision making as more extensive analysis. When past hurts are factored in, "thin slicing" may simply be a way to avoid dealing with hurt. Physiologically, "thin slicing" is akin to the bookie in your brain calculating the odds of success in the current event by looking at your track record in past events. The bookie has set the betting "line" for the problem and your intuition is now telling you to go for it or not. Are YOU satisfied with the decisions your bookie is making for YOU?

Think about your current level of hurt. Think about your current level of happiness. Is an adjustment in order? You can feel happier in the long run, if you are willing to deal with your pain differently in the short run. For instance, facing up to an uncomfortable situation in a relationship or at your job can help you to reestablish expectations and boundaries with your counterpart. While you may be frightened to say how you really feel, not saying how you feel can result in continuing pain. The choice is yours.

3) PAYOFFS FOR YOUR BEHAVIOR

Human behavior is NOT RANDOM. Your behavior makes sense at some level of your SELF CONCEPT. What you do and how you choose to live your life makes sense to you, actually benefits or rewards you, at some level. It's true that what may seem counterproductive to you is perceived as satisfying to someone else. This is equally true the other way around.

What hurts you may not even be noticed by others. What satisfies others may drive you crazy. Nevertheless, you have a unique set of payoffs or "PERCEIVED BENEFITS" that consciously or subconsciously drives your behaviors.

For instance, some people are obsessed with "keeping things in order." They must leave a clean desk at work each night or put their clothes away when they take them off at home or never leave dirty dishes sitting in the sink. Each of these behaviors has an apparent reward. A clean desk will cause others to think that the person is organized and disciplined in the way that they work, and having others think that way is important to this person. Sorting one's clothes and putting them where they belong (in the hamper or the closet) will help preserve the clothes and keep them in good condition. Keeping the sink clean may reduce the possibility of cockroaches invading the kitchen.

There is a good logical reason for all of these behaviors. But let's look underneath the logic at the emotional reasons (or the old scripts) that may be fueling these behaviors. It is one thing to engage in these behaviors 98% of the time. It is quite another to engage in them 100% of the time. At what point, are you driving the behavior? At what point is the behavior driving you?

Let's look at each of these behaviors through other possible filters. Perhaps the underlying reason is that we want to think that we have control over elements of our life. Although some of us seek control over things, people and outcomes, many other factors impact outcomes. Throughout the course of most of our lives, we are often just "pawns in the game of life."

At some point, we may settle for controlling elements in our immediate environment as a response to our perceived impotence at not being able to affect much of the outside world. You may not be able to control what your boss does or says nor what your customers may say, but you can feel satisfaction (the PAYOFF) at knowing that every single thing in and on your desk is as it is supposed to be.

Another possible payoff has to do with "criticism avoidance." As children, many of us were chided and criticized for being messy and not cleaning up after ourselves. Our brains noted how unpleasant hearing that scolding was. As a seven year old, putting things away was probably socially functional to keep peace within the family (particularly with your parents). However, some of us have forgotten the origins of that old script, and still continue the behavior with vague feelings of impending, ominous criticism if we discontinue the behavior. The PAYOFF back then was to avoid hassling with your parents or being punished. If your script is still the same, then it is fear of criticism that may drive the behavior, more than the desire to appear to be neat and organized.

To get in touch with YOUR PAYOFFS, take a good hard look at any behavior that you choose to do over 90% of the time. Ask yourself the following questions:

a) How long have I been doing this behavior?
b) When do I remember first doing this behavior?
c) Is there a person or event that I associate with this behavior?
d) Do I feel good when I do this behavior?
e) Did I always feel good when I did this behavior?
f) What might happen if I didn't do this behavior 100% of the time?
g) Is this behavior important to my SELF CONCEPT?
h) What other options are there for this behavior?
i) Have I ever tried any of these other options?
j) What happened when I tried the other options?
k) Is this behavior my choice or do I feel compelled to do this?

Thinking about these issues may uncover the PAYOFFS you have for continuing your behaviors. Just because you have uncovered your payoffs doesn't necessarily mean you should or will want to change your behaviors. You should just be able to look at these behaviors more honestly and hopefully more objectively.

Ask yourself if your current level of hurt is worth maintaining the behavior. How much is the behavior that you are engaging in impacting your life? If you are in a rush or really tired, does it matter if you put all of your clothes away or scour your sink? Are the payoffs for continuing to behave in this way worth it?

When a problem arises, you may be able to see the problem from more points of view if you are able to understand the payoffs that are driving your response or lack of response to the problem. Recognizing that your behavior is not random but somewhat orderly and/or predictable can help you to determine whether or not you want to change what you are doing and the levels of pain and happiness associated with it.

I have told many a "control freak" that if they want to have total control, there is only one real way to accomplish that. That is to become totally comfortable when everything is totally out of control, thereby giving up the need and illusion of control. Most control freaks are terribly unsatisfied with this, so they go back to cleaning their desks and sinks. At this point at least they are aware of the payoff that is driving the behavior.

4) ORDER, STRUCTURE, CONSISTENCY, RELIABILITY AND COHESION

You want the world to make sense to you. You are constantly engaging in pattern recognition at lightning speed at a cortical and sub-cortical level. Your brain strives to find a location for each piece of data it deems important. You are constantly making and changing synaptic connections to facilitate future decision making. Your life depends upon it, so the storage and accessibility of the data is a critical issue. After all, how could you ever decide what to do if you had to view each piece of information as if it was the first time you had encountered it?

Think about trying a new food. I remember eating at an Indonesian "rijstaffel" in Amsterdam. The waitress brought out 22 small dishes, each with a sampling of "food." The food had various textures, colors and appearance. First, I asked, "What is in each of these dishes?" It seemed important to me at the time to have an idea of what I was about to put into my stomach. The waitress replied, "Why don't you just taste it?"

I became all the more concerned. I wanted to make sure that I knew what I was about to eat. Seeing that I was going to get no help on this from the waitress, I proceeded to try each dish. Some were good, some were forgettable and some I would never eat again. But the first thing I noticed my mind doing was to attempt to categorize, sort and connect each of the dishes with other foods that I already was familiar with. In this way, I was able to quickly integrate these new foods into my mental food menu.

Think of the last time you ate a new food. Frog legs? Alligator? If you asked your food server what these items tasted like, you probably got the answer "chicken." Not so much because they taste exactly like chicken, but because chicken is listed inside your brain as a food that is palatable. That could allay your fears about trying that new food long enough to taste it.

The variance and elegance that separates the human brain from the most sophisticated computer is the system integration of these myriad pieces of data. Each single piece of data, each neuron, or each synapse (connection between neurons) may impact over a million other neurons or synapses in nanoseconds.

Data is constantly processed in parallel fashion, as opposed to serially. New data is compared to past experiences, and the internal brain bookie begins to set the odds board for new behaviors. The result of these transactions is a single, coordinated thought or action.

That said, when a pattern of behavior or thought has been set for a while (as in the case of traumatic or fear provoking data), one-time learning may be all that is required to impact behavior. You may become reluctant and even frightened to modify that behavior. This is particularly true when a potential new option conjures up past thoughts infused with FOF (Fear of Failure). Fear of Failure, which will be discussed in greater detail in Chapter 15, is often the single biggest reason preventing people from changing their behavior.

Structure and organization are necessary and useful to guide day-to-day functioning and decision making. However, they can also be immobilizing, when facing a new problem or challenge. You can become the proverbial "deer in the headlights" holding your ground as the onrushing car streams towards you. You can become frozen at times when you perceive that neither fight, nor flight, seems palatable.

Are you the kind of person who is endlessly prolonging and delaying action due to "analysis/paralysis?" If so, this book is designed to help YOU break out of that logjam.

5) CLOSURE

You seek CLOSURE about the events and thoughts in your life. If incomplete information is presented to you, your brain will attempt to synthesize completion in the least EMOTIONALLY DISRUPTIVE fashion. Speed and a return to your emotional well-being are much more important than logic itself. Being in limbo can be unsettling as you choose to integrate new information in the least disruptive way. New ideas or possibilities can be seen as threatening if they disrupt the well-being associated with the current organization of your brain.

Think about rumors and what happens when they spread. Think about urban legends that strike fear in your heart. Consider your reactions to unfounded frightening stories in the media or on the internet. The worst part of the rumors, urban legends and unfounded stories is the "trust gap" that is created. Suddenly you are less certain about where you stand. Current figures, once perfectly clear, now begin to cloud your mind as the background/context changes. Incomplete or unreliable data can unsettle and shake the very foundations of your belief system.

You want things to at least make emotional sense. Logical sense would be nice too, but keeping yourself calm and believing that you "understand what is going on" trumps knowing what is really going on. Even if you consider yourself a "very logical person."

Here is where credibility enters the picture and really matters. Think of two people whom you know. One person you perceive to be credible, the other person less credible. The "credible" person can say something to you that you know is a bit incorrect, but you will give this person the benefit of the doubt, mentally correct what they said and not let it impact their credibility with you (unless they do this repeatedly or deny doing this.) You still maintain emotional closure in your mind because there is a plausible explanation for the gap between what they said and what you believe.

The "non-credible" person can tell you the gospel truth with "facts" to back up what they say, but you still don't trust them in the same way. You will probably have a completely different interpretation of what was said. Despite the "facts" that they have presented, you will look for a hidden agenda or alternative interpretation and then reinterpret the facts or get your own facts to support what you believe. Ultimately, you will find not find them more credible, even if you admit that they may be right in this instance. If they start to do this consistently, you will have a real problem because it doesn't fit with your picture of who this person is and what they represent.

This raises another facet of our need to maintain emotional well-being. When we receive a piece of data that is dissonant or "out of whack" with what we believe, we struggle to make sense out of it.

Think of a person whom you don't like or trust. When that person suddenly does Activity A that is more advantageous to you than Activity B which is more advantageous to them, you find this puzzling. Here are several possible interpretations:

A) The person has changed and grown and is now a more caring individual.
B) It didn't really matter to the person as to whether he/she did Activity A or B.
C) This was really a set-up and they will try to get something in return later.
D) Maybe I should change my perception of this person and give them another chance to earn my trust.

Were you more swayed by explanation B & C than by A & D? Why? Perhaps you can see that accepting interpretation B or C allows you to keep your current perception of the other person intact, while interpretations A & D require you to reconsider your world view of that person. When hurt is involved, you can go to even great lengths to protect your SELF CONCEPT and picture of the world.

This book suggests that you can take lifelong scripts and hurts that have irked you for years and rise up from them. What is the easiest interpretation here?

A) This book offers real hope that I can live a happier life.
B) Like most other self-help books, this one promises things that can't be delivered. It all sounds good, but it is just too hard for me to do.
C) If I have success at rising up from my hurt, I may feel bad when I look back at all the time that I allowed myself to suffer. Possibly I will feel foolish that I didn't try this before.
D) I realize how hurt drives elements of my life. I also realize that if I don't do anything, my level of hurt will stay the same or get worse. I ought to try anything that potentially offers a happier life.

Were you again more swayed by explanation B & C, than by A & D? Once again, accepting interpretation B or C allows you to feel better about yourself and maintain your perception of yourself as a prudent person. Interpretations A & D require that you to reconsider your perception of how you have handled your hurt up to this point.

Psychologists label this phenomenon "cognitive dissonance." When your thoughts don't fit well together, you simply reorganize them so that they become consonant. If you look at how you process information, you will realize that you do this at times. You may call it rationalization, justification or use a whole host of other labels, but the process remains the same.

6) EMOTIONS AND LOGIC

Every sales person will tell you that you make decisions to buy an idea based more on your EMOTIONAL reaction to the idea than on your LOGICAL reaction to the idea. We have already described how the brain processes what we know about new ideas by first finding similar ideas you have come across in the past and referencing past pain and pleasure outcomes for those ideas. Then our brain provides an intuitive feeling (a sense that it is right) to your cortex which begins to THINK about the new idea based on old experiences.

What is critical here is that each new idea has an EMOTIONAL and LOGICAL aspect to it. In this book, I will ask you to look at the emotional side of an idea PRIOR to looking at the logical side. Why? You are more likely to buy ideas if you feel good about your possible options.

To make sure that you start your thinking from the best possible EMOTIONAL framework, you can learn to become an Option Thinker (Chapter 13.) As an option thinker, you should always start with a Best Case Scenario (BCS). If you think of a BCS first, it can raise your expectations and optimism about "what could be." Even if you don't use or accept a full blown BCS, just thinking along those lines first allows you to potentially integrate pieces of the BCS into the option you eventually select.

When hurt is involved, emotions do not always guide us to the best choices (particularly when we are dealing with a less than terrific track record when dealing with past hurts and failures.) When your brain prescreens new ideas for "hurt potential," it is easy to get frightened. It will be necessary for you to CAREFRONT those fears constantly in order to rise up from your hurt. Trying to rise up from hurt by using only logical options is more difficult than identifying, processing and reframing your emotional reactions to hurt.

7) INTENTION AND IMPACT

There is an interesting difference between the way you judge or evaluate yourself versus how you judge or evaluate other people. You judge yourself by your intentions. You are what you intend. However, since you don't have the same access to other people's intentions (you can only infer them), you judge others based on their impacts or outcomes of their intentions.

Here is a simple example. Imagine driving in your car and another driver cuts you off. Compare your reaction to when you cut someone else off. When you cut someone else off and they begin to develop a serious case of road rage, you are quick to absolve yourself of any culpability or guilt because you didn't intend to cut them off. It was an error in judgment on your part. Everyone should feel relieved because no one got hurt.

However, when other people cut you off, you know that they must have intended to do that. At the very least they were negligent, judgment impaired. Maybe they were texting at the time or just distracted. They didn't care that they scared you. They are probably a careless driver most of the time. They ought to at least be reprimanded and sent to driver's education classes. Heck, maybe they should have their license suspended or spend a few nights in county jail so that they wouldn't ever cut someone off again! A vastly different reaction to the same behavior.

You tend to be a lot more forgiving when you view our own behaviors compared to the behaviors of others. For some of us, our SELF CONCEPT is centered on what we intend.

What happens when our actions hurt others? We can be oblivious to how another person perceives our intentions. Jeff, who had been married twice, always believed that he was simply "helping" his wives when he made what he thought were helpful suggestions to them. Unfortunately, both of Jeff's wives perceived the HELP to be chronic "NAGGING" and put downs. He thought he was being "non-caring" IF HE DIDN'T say something about their potentially self-destructive behavior.

Jeff knew his intentions quite well. He sincerely wanted to help. He was less aware (his ex-wives would say "oblivious") to the impacts of his behavior. Jeff never was able to shift his perspective so that he could see it from their point of view.

Understanding the difference between intention and impact can help you better understand people's reactions to your actions. However, it can also help you to reframe the way you behave with yourself. You have no intention of hurting yourself. Just the opposite. You believe that you are coping with your hurt in the best possible way. But what are the impacts? If your hurt is causing you to live in an unhappy way, what should you attend to? Your intentions? Or your impacts?

Taking a good, honest hard look at your life should tell you what to do.

Chapter 5

RISING UP FROM HURT: GROUND RULES

In all the years that I have worked with people, it has become increasingly clear to me that once a person perceives that they have a "problem," they usually consider the issue(s) on the surface of the problem as the real problem. Do you do this? Like most logical people, once you have defined the problem in one way, you stop looking for other ways in which to see it. That is one reason why hurts typically don't get addressed correctly and why the hurt continues.

In working with couples, I have always explained that there tend to be 3 major issues that come up in any long-term committed relationship. When I speak about this in front of a large audience, I usually ask the men what their #1 issue is and almost instantly and without much prompting, a man will yell out "sex." Most of the other men in the audience will agree. When I ask the women what their #1 issue is, there is also fairly unanimous agreement when a woman yells out "money." No big surprises, so far.

However, when I ask for the third issue (and the one that really underlies all of the other issues), people start yelling out a wide variety of possibilities, including children, in-laws, details about their homes, jobs and how they spend their time. While all of these, on the surface, may seem important, I tell them the 3rd issue is really "Frank Sinatra." After the laughs and quizzical looks subside, I explain that the underlying issue that causes most marital problems is MY WAY -- power and control over who decides what will occur. If power is not somewhat evenly distributed during the relationship, the person who is not getting their way may have a problem.

It is so much easier to argue about which way the toilet paper is mounted on the roll in the bathroom or who holds the TV remote control unit than it is to discuss the issue of who makes most of the decisions.

Often whenever one person thinks and behaves as if they are in charge of the other person, resentment underlies the issue.

The toilet paper issue can be quickly resolved. One couple I know simply resorted to changing the direction of the roll from paper flying over the top to whipping out underneath EVERY TIME either of them went to the bathroom. But does it address what is really going on? Dealing with only the "tip of the iceberg" rarely prevents a catastrophic emotional collision when you are confronted with the true depth of feelings which lie underneath.

A few ground rules that may help you to move forward follow.

GROUND RULE #1

Be OPEN and HONEST with yourself as you look at your hurt. See what is really there. Hurts, like onions, have many layers to them. Focusing on only one layer may result in the problem recurring in another form.

Remember that, just because you see the problem one way, doesn't mean that is the only way to look at it. Poorly stated problems or problems viewed narrowly, in a myopic fashion, can result in frustration rather than in problem solution and personal growth.

You may have trouble being objective about what the hurt is. Maybe you can't tell the difference between a symptom of a bigger hurt and the hurt you are feeling right now.

Are you choosing not to face underlying issues, choosing to deal with the simpler surface issues? This can create the "short-term SMART, long-term NOT SO SMART" pattern which results in never really getting to the core hurt. You may need another more objective person to help you define the problem.

The goal is not to delay rising up from the hurt by doing mental gymnastics to see the problem from an infinite number of ways. The goal is to at least look at it from several different levels (start with 3 levels) and decide what you are willing to DO next.

GROUND RULE #2

There will be PAIN and DISCOMFORT when you change your behavior. Growth doesn't occur when everything is terrific. Growth can only happen when you are conflicted and CHOOSE TO ACT. Some of the problems that you have experienced have taken many years to develop. Patterns of behavior or scripts have been in place for a long time. There are few, if any, pain free methods that will magically and instantly change these long established patterns.

Consider how many people seek to lose weight through hypnosis, new diet fads or through machines that exercise your body for you. The lure of easy "pain free" behavior change is very attractive. People spend millions of dollars each year chasing fad after fad, in the hopes of avoiding PAIN. Consider the adage "If it sounds too good to be true, it probably isn't true."

Here is another one to consider -- "If it really worked that way, why wouldn't everyone be doing it?"

FACE IT. There will be PAIN. How much? What kind? That you don't know. But there will be PAIN. Accept that. Be assured too that all of that pain and hurt can be dealt with. Seek out people around you support you and help make it easier.

Ironically, those of you who are willing to step up and face your PAIN may have to deal with less of it. Those of you that shy away from pain are doomed to spend more time on the "treadmill of continual suffering."

GROUND RULE #3

Your SENSE OF URGENCY AND PERSISTENCE will be key determinants as to whether or not and how soon you hurt less. There has been much discussion recently concerning visualizing what you want to occur, the power of intention and the laws of attraction. While I think that positively viewing the changes that you want has value, the people who are successful in making changes are the people who want it so bad that they never stop going for it. They are that hungry for change. One successful person I know said it best: "I'm either going to get it done or you are going to find my dead body somewhere along the way."

So, HOW BADLY do you really want it? Why is today the day that you should start to deal with the "real" hurt? What will you do when the going gets rough? What will you do after you "slip up" for the first, second, or third time? It is particularly frustrating for people who have tried to solve their problem in countless ways before and have been less than successful.

Here is the key difference. In the past, when you have looked at your problem, you have simply tried to alter the behavior. Now behavior modification is important. All of the questions above and others must be addressed. This must be accomplished if your behavior has led you astray. BUT, in and of itself, it is not enough. Reframing of the hurt is what you need to make sure that you rise up and get beyond the hurt.

SHEILA

Sheila was a middle-aged woman who had just gotten divorced from her husband of 15 years. It had been a long time since she had gone out on a date with another man. At 42, she was now looking for the same kind of excitement and companionship that had been characteristic of the early years of her marriage. Since she had met her husband in a bar at age 25, she thought that she would start to bar hop again on Thursday nights, just to try it out and see how she felt. Bars have changed quite a bit in the past 15 years, as have the patrons and the "rules of conduct." Sheila tried to read a few books to help her get over her anxiety of "going out on dates again." She joined an on-line dating service and even found a "wing woman," Sally, to go with her, so she wouldn't have to be there alone. Sounds like Sheila should be on her way to meeting some new guys. Right?

Hold your horses. While Sheila has started to change her behaviors in some reasonable ways (the tip of the iceberg), has she taken the time to face any of the underlying issues for her divorce or to check in on her current readiness to date? Here are some things that Sheila might want to consider:

1) Why did her marriage end?
2) What did she do that contributed to the divorce?
3) What did her husband do that contributed to the divorce?
4) Who is she now?
5) How is she different from the woman who dated the last time at age 25?
6) What does she want/need in her life right now?
7) What does she want/need in her life from a man?
8) What is she prepared to give/not give to a new relationship?
9) Would some time spent alone be as valuable/more valuable as bar hopping on Thursday nights?

10) How can she avoid being swept up in a "rebound" relationship with the first man who shows her positive attention and affection?

What it really comes down to is that Sheila may first want to "reframe" her thoughts about her past hurts, her SELF CONCEPT, and what she really wants from a new relationship BEFORE she just goes out on dates. Doing so may result in the possibility of developing a more meaningful relationship with another man. Understanding the meaning of her divorce in her life and the hurt she endured is important. Sheila may realize that there are many more significant issues to deal with prior to dating again.

Understanding the meaning behind what you are doing and why you are attempting to change your behavior can help you to clarify your SENSE of PURPOSE and URGENCY. In Sheila's case, being alone for a while can be frightening; it can cause her to feel worthless and unwanted and lonely. Or perhaps it can be enlightening; it can help her to understand what she is doing on the planet and allow her to luxuriate in her new opportunity to rediscover who she is or wants to become.

People who are successful at hurting less choose to understand the context and meaning of what they are doing. They choose the right thing to do at the right time and use the clarity of vision and purpose to help them when they start to stumble.

Make sure you understand the meaning associated with your hurt BEFORE you just try to do something about it.

GROUND RULE #4

Authentic behavior CHANGE takes a while. I don't consider CHANGE to be real until it has endured for at least 3 weeks or 21 days. It takes that degree of consistency in the new behavior before it gains traction in your behavioral repertoire.

Many people would like to believe that they are out of the woods the very first time they do something different. That is not the case. The first time you modify your behavior, you may not have uncovered the "hidden payoffs" for your old behavior. Your excitement at embarking on your new course of action may smother deep feelings that underlie the behavior.

Another possibility is that you used "brute force" to get to the new behavior. In the heat of the moment, you went ahead without looking backward or considering what you were doing. You may have been lucky. You may have had an accidental success. Even though you may have even taken a step in the right direction, you may have done it for the wrong reason.

While you should truly celebrate your early successes, you shouldn't allow yourself to get carried away with them. You shouldn't think that you have avoided the pain and fear that usually accompanies behavior change. You shouldn't think that the hurt is over and done with. You should acknowledge the progress that you have made but realize that the path may have many potential pitfalls ahead.

Being realistic about this will allow you to be more forgiving of yourself if you should later stumble or lapse back to old behavior. There is nothing wrong with false starts, stumbles, errors, moments of weakness or other temporary setbacks. They are all par for the course.

However, if you have "reframed" the hurt correctly and created a sense of urgency and meaning about really wanting to change your behavior, then long-term change is likely and you can rise up from your hurt. Instead of "satisficing" (settling for something less than optimal), solving the real issue can help "maximize" your outcomes.

Enough with preliminaries already. Let's start to look at what is hurting you.

Chapter 6

WHAT HURTS YOU?

Now that is a really good question. Too many people simply define their hurt in terms of what is causing them immediate frustration or pain. Do you seek to describe your hurt in multiple ways or at several levels? Do you look at the problem in depth? Or do you prefer to stay at a surface level? If you could just get the immediate frustration or pain to go away, do you think that you would be done with your hurt?

Not so fast. The surface issue might go away only to be replaced by another, seemingly unrelated, problem.

CATHY

Consider Cathy and her description of her problem. Cathy was a 53-year-old, married mother of two teenaged girls, still living in the house with her husband Jim. Cathy and Jim were both successful people with good jobs. Cathy worked as a teacher in a middle school, while Jim was a buyer for an electronics company. They have both been employed at their jobs for more than 12 years. Their girls were busy with typical teenage activities, cheerleading, tennis, shopping, riding on emotional and hormonal roller coasters and falling in and out of love with teenage boys. They also had a dog named Buster, who completed the family.

Cathy described herself as very orderly; she managed to get most things done by creating routines for almost everything. Laundry was done on Tuesday and Friday. Food shopping occurred on Saturday morning with quick trips to the store when small items were needed. Cathy and Jim were both chronic list makers.

Cathy usually came home from school around 4:00 PM, got dinner started, checked the mail, took Buster out for a quick walk, fixed dinner and then sat down to grade papers and prepare materials for the next day at school. Jim got home later, so Cathy typically reheated dinner for him. They chatted briefly about their day, watched 1-2 shows on television and then started to get ready for bed.

But something was missing for Cathy. "During the week, my life is so completely structured from the morning till the evening. I start running at 6:15 AM and don't stop till I collapse after 8PM. I have no time to really do anything for myself. I am so busy taking care of my students, my husband, the girls and Buster that it seems I am just running on a treadmill and never really getting anywhere. The weekends aren't much better. Getting the girls to tennis, food shopping and doing the twelve million other things that I don't get to do during the week fills the weekend. Other than sleeping in for an hour on Sunday, there just isn't any "me" time."

When I asked Cathy what she would do if she had more time, she longingly said, "I'd love to read the stack of books on my nightstand, or take a Pilates class, do some gardening or even just write some poetry."

When I asked Cathy if she was hurting, she was somewhat surprised. She never connected the lack of "me" time with hurt. She just thought of it as the price she would have to pay until the girls were in college. When I asked her if she wanted to rise up from her hurt, she asked how I could help her get more time. That was the way she defined the issue. While that was one reasonable way to look at the issue, it was NOT the only way to look at it.

Let's consider a few other alternatives.

Jot down three other ways to describe the problem, before you read any further, to see if you can help Cathy possibly "reframe" her problem.

1)

2)

3)

Did you consider the issue from the following points of view?

Possibility #1
Cathy always believed that being a "good mother and good wife" meant that she was responsible to do all that she could to keep her husband,

children and Buster happy. That was a full-time job. Cathy also believed that being a "good teacher" meant that she was responsible to do all that she could to keep her students learning, engaged and happy. That was a second full-time job. Having 2 full-time jobs made it difficult to have "extra" time available for herself. Cathy had convinced herself that she would not be thought of as a good mother and a good teacher if she did not do everything that could be done for everyone around her.

If Cathy was willing to question her definition of a "good mother," "good wife," and "good teacher," she could possibly find more time for herself. Is a good mother one who does everything for her girls or someone who teaches and encourages them to do more for themselves? Even if Jim is tired and microwave challenged, does Cathy have to stop what she is doing to reheat his meal every evening? Could Cathy's students be trained to grade each other's papers? Is it critical that every paper be graded and returned immediately? And what about Buster? Can the girls take him for a walk every once in a while? Are the TV shows really worth the time it takes to watch them? Does Cathy have a DVR?

However, to Cathy, the definitions were givens. There were only two choices: good and bad. There was not much in between. Cathy was only looking at how to find more time for activities rather than at how she defined herself. If Cathy were to redefine the problem by reframing what a "good mother," "good wife," and "good teacher" are, she might have a more solvable issue and less hurt.

Possibility #2

Here is another way to look at what Cathy is going through. She thought that the key to solving the "not enough time" issue was to get better organized and to make more efficient routines. Like most list makers, Cathy loved to scratch things off her list. She felt a delicious sense of accomplishment as she plowed through her list. The most exciting times of her life occurred when items were scratched off the list and "the daily list" was almost completed. In fact, if she did something that was not on her list, she first had to write it on the list just so she could get the pleasure of scratching it off.

Here is the irony. Let's say Cathy has a 10-item list. Let's also say that she gets 9 of those items completed. In school, 9 of 10 would be an A. That would be quite an accomplishment. However, for Cathy, when she got down to 1-2 items on the list, it merely served as a prompt to start a new list. If she added 10 more items to the list, despite having done "A" caliber work, she now had a list of 12 items facing her the next day. It is hard to make real progress when you feel that you are slowly slipping into the quicksand. It is impossible to find time for yourself because that rarely, if ever, makes it onto the list. Therein, lies another way to look at the problem.

It was NOT a time management issue at all. It was a Priority Management issue. If getting things done on the list trumps time for yourself ALL OF THE TIME, is there any surprise who gets stuck with the short end of the stick?

If Cathy were to look at the priorities in her life, she might realize that taking care of herself, relaxing, reading or writing poetry would be more important than getting a few more errands done.

At the end of people's lives, people rarely complain about not having completed more items on their "To DO" lists. They wistfully say that they should have spent more time laughing, smiling, smelling the roses and just being in the moment. Too bad this wisdom comes to most people at the end of their life as opposed to when they can still do something about it.

For Cathy, she may choose to reframe her conceptions of selfishness vs. selflessness and the guilt associated with being selfish. Is it selfish and unacceptable to spend time taking care of yourself? OR can you really take better care of others (students, husbands, girls and Buster) if you take care of yourself first? If Cathy gives herself permission to look at her old script, check out her SELF CONCEPT and her priorities, she may see that time isn't the issue at all. Her choices of what is important and what is "acceptable" are the issue.

Cathy is choosing to spend so much time WORKING for herself and others, that there isn't much time or energy left for PLAY, which leads us to yet another level of the problem.

Possibility #3

Cathy grew up in a religious family where she was told that "idle hands were the devil's playground." Cathy's mother, Esther, instilled the idea that strong "god fearing" women were the ones who worked hard to give their families all the bounties that they could afford. She watched her own mother and father work hard all day, almost every day when she was growing up in Iowa. Taking time out to just sit down was considered wasteful. If you were going to sit down, there were always plenty of things you could do while you were sitting there. She could never remember her father "just sitting and doing nothing." Cathy accepted this script and description of a "good woman" and never gave it another thought. Now it drives her behavior every day with the accompanying angst that Cathy does not have enough time to ever live her life just for herself.

Though Cathy is not a religious woman today, she had never really thought about how this old script governs her life today. Is it really "bad" to just sit? Will she get scolded and frowned upon if she does that? Will she immediately start to feel guilty about not doing something "more worthwhile" with her time? Here again, her concept of what is "good" and what is "bad" and the guilt associated with making the wrong choices underlies the issue of how to spend her time.

Possibility #4

Let's try one more way to see this. Cathy described herself as a "high energy" person. She said she liked being busy and felt good when she was being productive. All well and good. Could she feel equally good, just sitting and enjoying a sunset? Maybe, but Cathy never gave herself a chance to do that. Some people that say they like being really busy are actually not all that fond of being really busy. They are just avoiding something that they perceive to be a lot worse. Like what? Like BOREDOM.

I know several people who are so afraid to slow down and "do nothing" because they can't imagine anything more painful than having "nothing to do." Their imagination is that they will be wasting time and that the inactivity will be maddening. Not so fast.

What may underlie this thought process may be something totally different. Imagine taking a day and just sitting somewhere beautiful. No books. No music. No phone. No IPAD. No one around, except you. To some people this sounds like an idyllic day. To others this is a day fraught with danger.

What is the danger? Well, if you are not that busy with things to do, you might find that some deeper, previously hidden thoughts can find their way to the surface. Not everyone is comfortable with introspection and the Confrontation/Carefrontation with old memories, scripts or thoughts about themselves.

Some people create such a jam packed schedule, not because they like the hectic pace. They do it to avoid something else that they perceive to be more painful. A clean garage may be the sign of a "sick" mind. Is there anything Cathy could be trying to avoid?

CHOOSING A VIEW

So which problem statement will Cathy use to define her issue?
1) a "not enough time" issue
2) a "good mother/good teacher" vs. "bad mother/bad teacher" issue
3) a priority management issue
4) a "selfish" vs. "selfless" issue
5) a work-play ratio issue
6) an "idle time is non-productive time" issue
7) a "boredom" phobia issue
8) a "fear of learning about myself" issue?

Cathy has to make a choice as to which issue and what level of hurt she is willing to work on. Some involve surface changes/options, while others open up the door to a deeper "What am I doing on this planet?" type of inquiry.

How many of the problem statements listed above did you think of when you wrote down your 3 problem statements? Did you find other ways to see the problem that weren't mentioned? If you were Cathy, which problem looks the easiest for you to solve?

We will revisit Cathy's situation in Chapter 13 on Option Thinking.

Now, take a few moments to identify a particular issue in your life. What is your comfort level in addressing these types of issues? While you may not have Cathy's particular issue, you may find that your situation can also be viewed from a variety of vantage points as well. Can you come up with different ways to look at them? Write those here:

1)

2)

3)

Do any of them seem to resonate with you more than others?

BRUCE

Consider Bruce and his description of his issue. Bruce was 34, and Emily, his wife, was 32. They had been married for 9 years. They were college sweethearts and had lived together for 2 years before tying the knot. They did not have children yet, but they said they wanted a "big family." They moved from their hometown of Pittsburgh, PA to Palo Alto, CA because Bruce got a great job offer from an exciting start-up company. They both worked and made a reasonably good living. Since they were new to Palo Alto, they hadn't made many friends yet and had no family nearby.

Friday night used to be movie night when they would come home from work, order dinner in, microwave buttered popcorn, catch up and reconnect with one another. It was a tradition that they kept weekly for over 3 years. Lately, Bruce began stopping by a local bar on the way home on Fridays and getting home later and later. One week, he got so drunk at the bar that he had to call Emily to have her pick him up since he didn't think he could drive himself home safely.

Emily had started to go the gym more regularly during the week, taking Zumba dancing and yoga classes and even had started to go hiking every Saturday with a group of women she met at the gym. They often cleaned up after the hike and went to the local mall to have lunch and window shop afterwards.

Intimacy issues began to arise. There was less frequency to their intimacy, and Bruce complained that he thought they were in a rut, just going through the motions. Lately, Bruce found himself looking at younger women in the office, wondering what it would be like to be with them, instead of being with Emily. For the first time, he thought that maybe he should have gone out with more women before he got married. He hadn't told Emily about this because he was afraid to "hurt her feelings." He hadn't asked Emily how she was feeling about the relationship because he "wasn't sure he really wanted to know the answer." When asked what the issue was, Bruce said, "I don't feel the same way about Emily as I did when we got married. And I'm not sure she feels the same way about me. We're like an old married couple, with a boring sex life, just living together like roommates. I need more excitement in my life."

Well, that's one way to look at it. Maybe it is just the 7-year itch that impacts many relationships. Maybe Bruce and Emily had just fallen out of love. If Bruce doesn't see any other way to view the issue, he may be on the verge of doing something he may regret as a way of coping with his growing unrest.

Jot down three other ways to describe the problem, before you read any further, to see if you can help Bruce possibly "reframe" his problem.

1)

2)

3)

Bruce defined the issue as needing "more excitement" in his life. That is certainly one reasonable surface level description of the frustration he feels. He thought he was dealing with this issue when he drank at the bar more than he used to and when he fantasized about dalliances with other women that he worked with. Both of these options could, in fact, bring more excitement into his life and relief from the frustration he feels, in the short term. But they also could bring a host of possible long-term issues, the most significant one being the destruction of the trust and respect bond between Bruce and Emily.

How else can we view the problem?

Possibility #1

Bruce moved from Pittsburgh with Emily and left behind a huge support system of friends and family. All of the energy that Bruce used to divide among his buddies and family was now being drawn back into himself. He had not found other outlets for this energy that worked well within the relationship. He was now depending on Emily to be his friend, lover, confidant and wife. On top of that, he was expecting her to be aware of his thoughts, without having told her anything about the way he was feeling.

Bruce's father, Len, was a man on the go, all of the time. He had plenty of friends at the bars he frequented after completing his shift as a forklift operator for a local retail store. He also was quite popular with other women at work and with those women that were regulars at the bars as well. Bruce was not sure if Len had ever actually cheated on his mother, but he certainly had his suspicions. He often overheard his mother ask questions about Len's whereabouts whenever he came home exceptionally late or drunk. Bruce's picture of a "regular guy" was largely formed through the influence of his father. Bruce never questioned what it meant to be a "man." He was sure that he knew.

Like many men, Bruce chose to communicate using "telepathy." He didn't share his feelings of angst with Emily, yet expected her to "know how he felt." One way to "reframe" the issue has to do with what to do with all of the bottled up energy that he had. Could it be used to find new friends or find another type of support (other than the bottle or a younger woman)?

Bruce was attributing the lack of sexual excitement to Emily, without her awareness of this. His fantasy was that modifying their bedroom behavior or engaging in mental fantasies about other women would satisfy his "need for excitement." Maybe for a short while, it would. However, he had not yet considered that the issue may have as much to do with "lack of connectedness" as it does with "lack of excitement."

Consider that in most marriages, a classic complaint is that "you're not the man/woman whom I married." This is often said as a critique. The appropriate answer to this jibe should be "Thank goodness. I/we have both grown. Did you expect me to stagnate at the same place for the rest of my life?" Growth is a great and natural part of life. (And remember that one of the greatest facilitators of growth is conflict.)

Emily had made new friends and taken an interest in the gym, Zumba dancing, yoga and hiking. She was getting some support from these new friends as well. She was starting to grow in some different directions. All of these directions appeared to be healthy and not in conflict with growing her marriage.

Bruce, on the other hand, had not tried as many new things that could give him the sense of adventure and excitement that he sought. There is a well-noted difference between the East Coast and the West Coast in terms of "friend" relationships. East Coasters tend to have fewer friends but are more likely to have a deep connection with them. They tend to maintain these friendships over longer periods of time and distance. West Coasters often have more "acquaintances" but with less depth and less durability. Some of this is driven by the fact that many East Coasters are born and raised and remain in the same general communities that they grew up in. West Coasters tend to be more transient and on the move. Friendships that blossom in later years may not have the same durability as those relationships which had their origin during formative childhood or teenage years. Some people who "cross the Mississippi" don't realize this and generally have a hard time adjusting to what they perceive as the differences in making and keeping friends.

Bruce could have sought the excitement that he craved by adjusting his concept of "making friends" beyond those that he shared drinks with on Friday nights. At the outset, hanging out with new friends may not be as exciting as hanging out with old friends. It takes time to build the camaraderie, the inside jokes and the other "bonding" factors that create intense relationships. However, Bruce had to start somewhere.

Possibility #2

Here is another way to see the problem. Perhaps the issue was not really sexual excitement at all, but more centered on what was meaningful in their relationship. Bruce used to describe his love and affection for Emily in terms of 5 factors:

1) They could talk to each other about everything. They never ran out of things to say to one another.

2) They shared core values and could understand each other's feelings. They had empathy for another. If Emily was hurting, Bruce would know, care and be there for her. This was equally true if Bruce was hurting.

3) They spent a lot of time just laughing together. Laughter was always a pleasing sound that made them feel closer to one another.

4) There was a strong physical attraction and connection between them. They both could stare at each other for long periods of time thinking about how lucky they were to have each other.

5) There was a willingness to "mutually sacrifice" for one another. If Bruce really wanted something, Emily would "accommodate his wants and desires," just because she knew how much it meant to him. Bruce would also accommodate Emily when she really wanted something.

Bruce had chosen to focus on the "lack of intimacy" as the hub issue underlying his feelings. Bruce had ignored the fact that he had chosen not to talk with Emily about how he felt. He had not given her a chance to empathize with him. He had not given her a chance to "sacrifice" on his behalf because she was largely unaware of what was going on.

Adding creative elements to intimacy and "spicing" things up in the bedroom could be a positive element in changing how Bruce was feeling in the short term. Sexuality can be thrilling and exciting for many years. However, it may be difficult to keep things perpetually lively if the other areas are not addressed concurrently.

As couples evolve through time, the ways in which they maintain a relationship, what they see and define as important, can shift dramatically. For many couples, youthful lust that was once felt as vital may now become overshadowed by the need for companionship and understanding. The irony is that by concentrating on companionship, care and concern, the fires of intimacy can be stoked to new levels. It is not just women who need dialogue and caring. Men (even those that don't like to admit it) can crave it as well.

Possibility #3

Perhaps Bruce is just dealing with midlife issues such as "Is that all there is?" Many of these crises are indeed "crises of Meaning." Bruce may be a bit young to be going through midlife issues, but he manifests the itchiness, uncertainty and internal questioning that is typical of mid-life self-evaluation.

For his whole life, Bruce's definition of success centered on having a great career, earning a six-figure income, having a wife and family and living in a nice home. All of these goals were admirable and appropriate for a person with Bruce's upbringing.

Those values had been instilled in him by his family, friends and acquaintances in Pittsburgh. That was the script that he had written for himself while he was growing up. Now at age 34, perhaps it would be good for Bruce to reconsider how he wants to define "success." Is it time for a redefinition? Life for some people in their 30's begins to take on new dimensions. The early part of a man's life may be devoted to making an impact in the world and proving himself. Bruce was indeed a hard driver who sought to prove himself every day and every night. He was the sort of driven soul that was persistent in everything he did. On his way to work Bruce would count the number of cars he passed on the highway each day and kept track. He knew what his "record" was and was always trying to beat it. That competitive edge served him well in many arenas.

However, perhaps a definition of success that focuses exclusively on numbers, doing better and better and constantly proving himself needs some mellowing or tempering. Perhaps what was once exciting could evolve into another level of gratification that was even more profound. It might become more centered on who Bruce is and who Bruce yearns to become as opposed to how much he has accomplished.

Every day can be perceived as an adventure or exciting if we allow ourselves to focus on the profound beauty that surrounds us or on our connection with a higher power or a global community.

Considering "Is that all there is?" may indeed become a very exciting quest for Bruce because he is pioneering new uncharted territory. The inner journey could be as thrilling as front seating a roller coaster at Six Flags. It may also deepen his relationship with Emily because their love may be able to grow into areas that they have not paid attention to recently.

CHOOSING A VIEW

Like Cathy, Bruce has to make a choice as to which issue and what level of hurt he is willing to work on. Some involve surface changes/options, while others open up the door to a deeper "What am I doing on this planet?" type of inquiry.

Which problem statement will Bruce use to define his issue?
1) a "lack of excitement" issue
2) a reallocation of energy that used to go in "other directions" issue
3) a need for new friends or support group issue

4) a difference in personal growth between Emily and himself issue

5) a "what aspect of our relationship is most important right now: communication vs. empathy vs. intimacy" issue

6) a preview of mid-life issues (such as "what is my definition of success) issue

7) an "is that all there is?/ what is my place in the cosmos" issue.

It is evident that Bruce can choose to address this problem on a more mundane or on a more spiritual level. He can choose to deal with this alone (as he is currently doing) or choose to invite Emily to help him and to use the problem as a growth vehicle to deepen their relationship He can choose to deal with the issue and the underlying hurt associated with it on a deeper more meaningful level or continue to sit in a bar and lift nothing heavier than a 16-ounce adult beverage.

What is critical here is to recognize *how many ways there are* to see the issue and the hurt. The more ways in which we can view it, the more options that become available to solve it, which we will discuss later in Chapter 13 (Option Thinking). Bruce can choose to change his level of excitement or he can choose to change his life.

At the beginning of this chapter after I introduced you to Cathy, I asked you to identify a particular issue that was causing some pain in your life and to see if you could come up with different ways of framing the matter.

Take a moment to review your notes above. Spend some time again reflecting on your thoughts: Do you want to change your view of your issues? Will you choose to stay at the surface and deal the your issues in the short run or have you reached the point where you are willing to dig deeper, rise up from your hurt and pursue a happier life?

Chapter 7

PAYOFFS FOR CHOOSING TO STAY HURT

When people have hurt, they have payoffs or benefits for retaining that hurt. It is critical for you to discover, own and understand your payoffs for deciding whether or not to rise up from your hurt. There are payoffs for both choices.

In the 1970's, I taught a community college personal growth class called "Enjoying Your Depression." This class was taught well before the contemporary views of depression, which stress the role of chemical imbalances, came into vogue. Therefore, I tended to focus on other, more psychological, factors that could be causing and perpetuating depression and the pain associated with it. The class was offered as a personal and educational growth class more than as a therapeutic class.

You can imagine what the people who attended a class with this title were hoping for. It was very reminiscent one of the most troubling game shows ever to be broadcast on television. Older readers may remember a game show called "Queen for A Day." On this show, three women were invited to share some of the difficulties of their lives. At the conclusion of the show, after much cathartic release, a robe and tiara was placed on one of the contestants as she was proclaimed Queen for the Day. She usually received a kitchen appliance, such as a refrigerator or an oven as her reward.

The gift itself was ironic to me since her problem often had to do with having a husband who was out of work or children who were causing trouble at home; receiving a refrigerator or oven was not likely to help this woman deal with any of those problems. The contestant did receive some empathy and sympathy from the audience and host's faux comforting words to her plight.

In any event, many of the people who enrolled in the class were not unlike the contestants on the show – each hoping to find a way to alleviate the pain and the hurt that they felt.

My class was held over two weekends on a Friday evening and a Saturday morning. Each of the 20-30 students could receive 1 unit of credit for attending the class. The majority of the attendees were women, but there were always a good number of men as well. On the first Friday evening, after I would briefly introduce myself, I would ask each person to stand up, tell us their name and what they were unhappy about.

Some people had experienced very difficult circumstances ranging from illness to death of a spouse to job loss. Although the class offered a certain amount of sympathy as each person spoke, an interesting trend developed. The level of severity of the problems presented seemed to increase dramatically as we went around the room. However difficult the first person had it, the people who spoke later always seemed to have a more traumatic issue to contend with. It was as if they knew they would not receive a maximum amount of sympathy if all they were depressed about was similar to what another participant had already said.

After each person had identified their issue, I did remind the attendees that the title of the class was "ENJOYING Your Depression." I started to ask people if they could identify any benefits for staying depressed. After all, what good did it do for them to continue to be depressed?

At first, the students looked at me as if I were kidding. There weren't any benefits to being depressed, they thought. How could I be so heartless as to suggest that they were benefitting from their difficulties?

I started to point out a few possibilities:

1) When we are depressed, we don't focus as much on our appearance because we just don't care or don't have to energy to do so. I suggested that people come to class the next day dressed however they felt -- in pajamas, with hair curlers, without make-up, without showering or dressed in whatever made them just feel comfortable.

2) I also suggested that, when we are depressed, many of us allow ourselves to eat "comfort foods." Since we are not so excited about life or our appearance, at least we can get a little happiness from eating foods that we like. I suggested that people should feel free

to bring food that they enjoyed to class the next day and eat it. If they were going to bring food, I asked them to bring enough to share with at least one other person in class.

3) When we are depressed, we have a good reason/excuse not to do certain things. After all, "who cares if I do those things anyway?" If I am always tired and sad, there is no reason to exercise or clean up after myself, pay bills on time or meet some of other more challenging responsibilities. I asked people to bring their "To Do" lists to class to share with one another and see what activities were being postponed most often.

4) If we are depressed, we expect other people to feel sorry for us and do things to make us feel happy. If they don't do these things, then we have proof that they didn't really know/love us in the first place. We, in turn, don't have to do that much for them. I asked people to think of at least one other person in the room that they might want to chat with the next day in the hopes that they would lend a sympathetic ear (or at least share their food.)

5) When we are depressed, we often feel tired and sleep more. It may be easier to live in the "world of dreams" than in reality. In the dream world, people may get an escape from the drudgery of depression. I suggested that if students wanted to bring pillows, they might choose to take a little nap if and when they found that the class got boring.

Students began to look at me with the look of "Wait a Minute here. I've been had." They initially thought that I was making fun of them when, in fact, nothing could have been further from the truth.

The whole point of the discussion was to introduce them to the concept of "payoffs." Before you can DO ANYTHING to change your situation and deal with an issue involving hurt, you need to understand what is driving you to hold onto your current behavior. For some of the students with very difficult issues, such as death of a spouse or a child, they may have done nothing to bring about/cause the situation. However, if a reasonable amount of time has passed (which varies for each person), there may be payoffs for choosing to stay within the grief as opposed to moving on.

BARB

One woman in class, Barb, felt very bad about the fact that her husband had suddenly died two years earlier from a pulmonary embolism. One moment he was sitting there laughing with her; the next moment he was dead and gone. Barb still wore her wedding band proudly and had not considered herself ready to date again.

I asked Barb what payoffs she had for "not wanting to date." I asked her if she thought that her husband would have wanted her to date after he had died. Barb thought carefully and then said that he probably would have encouraged her to do so. She thought that she was still attractive, but, upon further questioning, it was clear that she was concerned about the possibility of being rejected by potential dates. She was also concerned about being out of touch with current dating practices, standards and expectations (sexual, romantic and familial). It seemed that the possibility of being rejected was more frightening to her than the opportunity to find another "love of her life."

Barb also began to realize that she was quite traumatized by the loss of her husband. It reminded her of her childhood concerns about abandonment. Both of these experiences presented a lot of very painful feelings for Barb to process. As a child, her father had left her family when she was quite young and never returned. She was raised by her mother, who never remarried. She couldn't even remember whether or not her mother had ever gone out on a "date" after that. The thought of losing another man after the loss of her father and husband was just too much to bear. Instead, Barb had chosen to live with her memories of her husband, unwilling to take any more chances extending her heart. It had been easier for Barb to have the "problem" of dealing with remaining single rather than having the problem of not yet having let go of early childhood issues.

As the class concluded, Barb realized that she would have to consider "reframing" her past thoughts about abandonment before she could ever successfully date another man. What had started off as an issue about current dating protocols became a much deeper consideration about her level of trust in men and the possibility that she would be abandoned again.

SID

Sid knew that he had a very bad temper. When things did not go the way that he wanted, he would loudly protest to the point of ranting at whoever would listen. Sid kept telling everyone that the world wasn't fair. He thought he was always drawing the short straw in life. My telling him that "a fair is where pigs win medals" didn't get much of a smile from Sid. He fully had an expectation that his God should rectify any imbalances that occurred in his life immediately. He could not understand why things never seemed to balance out for him. He thought he was entitled to be angry, but he was also sad at times because most people did not care to be around him when he was angry or sad. Of course, what underlies most anger is hurt. Sid could see the anger but chose not to recognize that he was hurting as well.

When asked what his payoffs were for his anger, Sid could not immediately see anything good that derived from his behavior. When I pointed out that he valued the victim stance, he initially objected. However, he soon saw that his concept of "fair" extended beyond this lifetime. Sid felt that if God was not helping to restore balance on earth, perhaps he would do so in the afterlife. Sid believed that he would get his just rewards at some point.

Another possible payoff for Sid was that people left him alone. Although he said he was sad when people did not want to be around him, he also enjoyed his time alone. When he was alone, there was no one to disagree with him or more importantly to disappoint him. When our persona has little control over others and their reactions to us, it may be safer to be alone and maintain control over how we see the world. People certainly gave Sid space and would not ask him to do things when he was angry.

The angry feelings masked the hurt. Anger and hurt are closely related. Anger is the external manifestation of internal hurt. Men, in particular, are much more comfortable dealing with their anger, while often denying that they are hurt at all. As long as he focused on being angry, he could maintain his "stiff upper lip," and see himself as a "man's man." A "man's man" doesn't get hurt. Having a stiff upper lip may give the illusion of control. However, underneath that façade are feelings that are buried. Having a stiff upper lip causes men to get sick and die younger. In Sid's case, in order to preserve Sid's image of himself as a man "who didn't take crap" from anyone, his anger would rage. At times, he would become severely depressed, which he wrote off as an entirely appropriate reaction to the "unfair" world that he lived in.

Stop here. Spend some time working through the problem you identified in the previous chapter. What possible payoffs might you have for holding onto this particular problem?

Fear of Failure (FOF)

At times we hold onto a problem, because having the problem is BETTER than the unknown feelings that accompany having to do something about it. The FOF can be so strong that it stands in the way of taking any action at all.

Many people spend entirely too much time looking for options to issues where:

1) They don't have to DO anything.
2) Other people will do all of the changing.
3) Other people will take the blame/bear the consequences of options that don't work out.
4) A miracle occurs, and the issue just goes away.
5) Time passes, and the issue just goes away on its own.
6) There is a book they can read that will make it easy to solve the issue.
7) There is an easy, no-risk option that is guaranteed to work.
8) They will fully understand the issue and can logically map out options that will eliminate risk.
9) There is no chance to fail.
10) A divine power will intercede on their behalf.
11) The world will magically return to the condition it was in prior to the issue. As a child we always wanted a "do over" when the game didn't go as we expected it.

Good luck if you are waiting for any of these options to occur. Buy lottery tickets. Pray. Hope. Wish. Do all of those things. If good fortune is with you, maybe something will happen. For the rest of us, it is up TO US TO DO SOMETHING DIFFERENT THAN WE HAVE DONE BEFORE.

The payoffs for doing nothing can be quite strong. As tough as the situation may seem, at least it is a known situation. We know the kind and amount of pain and hurt that we are in. Even though we don't like it, it isn't likely to kill us. We can acclimate to it if we distract ourselves enough. The unknown, on the other hand, can be "catastrophized" into a truly horrible scenario. We can imagine all kinds of frightening, embarrassing and failure-filled experiences, any of which will keep us from moving forward and rising up from our hurt.

Consider the following payoffs for doing nothing. Do any of these ring true for YOU?

1) It is too hard to change. There may be pain.
2) I may not be able to change.
3) It takes too much effort.
4) It takes too much time.
5) I don't know how.
6) There is nothing that I (or anybody else) can do to make the situation better.
7) There are no solutions.
8) This is a better problem to have than other problems that could be associated with trying to change (Fear of Failure of another type.)
9) I am embarrassed to admit that I have this problem.
10) It isn't really a problem. It is the path that God has chosen for me.
11) I deserve having this problem. It is payback for other bad things I have done.

Is there any wonder that people do not jump at the chance to rise up from their hurt? It would seem at first glance that it is much easier to do nothing than to deal with the unknown of what could come next. Most people will not make the decision to give up a payoff unless they feel somewhat certain that they can attain an even greater payoff.

Before you can rise up from your hurt, you will have to identify the payoffs you have for holding on to your issue. Not addressing this issue or denying that you have any payoffs for holding onto your hurt will only result in delays in rising up from your hurt.

A good place to start looking at your payoffs is to consider the deprivations in your life. Deprivations often breed motivations. What you have been deprived of determines what you want or need. Think about that for you. What deprivations do you have? How have those deprivations contributed to your behavior? For instance, if you grew up without much money, you might hoard it when you get older. If you grew up out of the limelight, you might now seek the spotlight whenever you can.

Perhaps you will choose a behavioral symptom to change without getting to the deeper issues (possibly resulting in the problem reappearing in another form).

Maybe you will just decide that you don't need to understand what underlies the problem in order to rise up from your hurt. There are many mental health professionals who believe that the behavior is the ONLY problem and that if the behavior is changed, there is little else to be concerned about.

As you continue reading, I hope you will develop a sense of optimism and possibility. I hope that you will choose to take action and change your life.

Chapter 8

PAYOFFS FOR RISING UP FROM YOUR HURT (THE FLIP SIDE)

The intention of this BOOK is to become an UNBALANCING FORCE IN YOUR LIFE and to invite you to change your life. That is what is at stake here. CHANGING YOUR LIFE! It is about beginning to seize control of things that you have allowed to interfere with living your life to its fullest. It is about carpe diem. It is about taking the first step towards seeing opportunities for growth, instead of seeing insurmountable problems. It is about much more than the current issue which brought you to read this book. It is potentially about LIVING A DIFFERENT LIFE!

The first step is to fire up your imagination as to what your life will be when you rise up from your hurt. Imagine the FREEDOM! Imagine the POSSIBILITIES!

What could you do with the energy that you are currently using to contend with your hurt? How could that energy be reinvested in you, your family, your friends, your career or in whatever direction you choose?

Here are some possible payoffs that may motivate you to rise up from your hurt:

1) Developing a supreme sense of accomplishment at having completed something very challenging and difficult,
2) Feeling physically better,
3) NOT having to spend psychic and physical energy maintaining escape behaviors,
4) Using what you have learned to deal with this hurt to help rise up from other hurts,
5) Seeing yourself more honestly and with a more optimistic perspective,
6) Growing as a person,

7) Being more loving and accepting towards yourself and others,

8) Taking the extra energy that you were using to avoid dealing with the hurt and doing something exciting with it,

9) Having more success in the world,

10) Serving as a better role model to your family, friends and coworkers,

11) Setting new higher level goals and possibly reaching those goals as well,

12) Being HAPPIER!

When you compare the payoffs in this chapter versus the last chapter, it doesn't seem like much of a choice, does it? Understanding that there are payoffs for everything, wouldn't you rather go with boundless energy and possibilities?

It just seems so obvious that trying something new is better than the status quo. If preserving the status quo were true, I wouldn't be writing this book. There would be little need for therapists, counselors and coaches.

Payoffs for making no changes are often chosen because of the way in which people view potential levels of pain, effort and persistence needed, fate, karma and a host of other factors. Logic is often not enough to spur action. Emotions and our history of problem solving and past failures weigh in very heavily when we make our choices. Do not underestimate their influence.

Remember that YOU DO HAVE THE CHOICE! That is what I hope you realize at this point. That is new. Until this point, you may have felt like you were a victim of your own circumstance. Now you have the opportunity to make the call:

Keep the hurt I have

OR

DARE to DO something different about it.

At the very least, I hope YOU will take responsibility for the choice that YOU are currently making. If you are choosing NOT to DEAL with your hurt in a proactive manner, understand your payoffs for doing so.

Compare your list of payoffs from the last chapter with those listed in this chapter. What do you see? Which direction do you want to take?

This greater level of self-awareness and understanding can be helpful to you, even if YOU do not choose to make any changes in your life at this time. At least, YOU will have a different perspective on what YOU are doing. In the long run, YOU may be more open to doing something different at a later point.

However, if FOF is what's standing in your way, I urge you to take the CHANCE OF A LIFETIME AND CHOOSE TO LIVE with *at least one less hurt* in your life. I can urge you until I am blue in the face, but I have learned one thing from working with people with FOF (Fear of Failure). The only antidote to FOF is success. I can talk about building confidence, practice, using the correct tools, but it all comes down to this:

> You will only believe that you can succeed once you have had a taste of success. One success may or may not be enough. Repeated success may be necessary to convince you that the hurt can be reframed.

Here is the irony: You can't have those repeated successes until you at least get started. You will have to take the plunge, while still feeling anxious, uncertain or itchy. It can start as a matter of faith, belief, hope or prayer, but if you are fortunate, you can rise up from your hurt.

Ready? Have you decided to rise up from your hurt?

Let's turn our attention then to how you can martial your sense of urgency.

Chapter 9

DEVELOPING YOUR SENSE OF URGENCY

Today is just another day in the rest of your life. That is true for almost all of us. On a typical day in the United States, between 5,000 and 6,000 people die. They no longer have the luxury of putting off until tomorrow what could/should be done today. For those people who know they are dying, today is usually urgent.

Other people who also have a sense of urgency include people who have been diagnosed with a terminal illness, people who have had a life threatening experience (such as an accident or brush with death) or people who have experienced the death of someone close to them. It often takes an encounter or heightened awareness of your own mortality to put things in perspective.

In my work with dying people, I have been struck by their approach to life. Those that are lucid and can still communicate become focused on what is immediate and matters to them. For many of them, life becomes centered on what there is to eat, how to mitigate their pain and how to remain comfortable in their surroundings. That is what matters most to them. That is what they focus their attention on.

One of my dearest friends, who recently died from COPD (Chronic Obstructive Pulmonary Disorder), had become thrilled with nature photography. He constantly looked for opportunities to take pictures of the animals and birds that frequented the area around his home. He had taken unusual delight in framing those pictures and giving them away to people that he interacted with. By doing so, he ensured that a piece of him and his legacy would live on. This is what he focused his attention on.

Most people take each day for granted and don't feel obligated to push themselves to their limits until trauma occurs to them or someone close to them. When I worked with people in this category in therapeutic sessions, I was often surprised that, even when they were in obvious pain, they seemed to be in no rush to alleviate that pain. At times, all I could say to them was "I guess you just need more pain before you are really ready to do something about it." This saying seemed empty as I said it, but there was some truth to it. Some people were simply not ready to consider change until they reached what they considered to be the "point of no return."

When I talk to people who have a sense of urgency about a hurt that has not been created by trauma, it becomes clear that they have "reframed" an experience or set of experiences. That fuels their single-minded focus and attention when it comes to dealing with hurt.

Allow me to offer a few examples of rising up from hurt in my own life. It is clear to me that dealing with hurt is more natural to individuals who have experienced their fair share of pain.

THE "GIFT OF HURT" IN MY LIFE

Hurt can be seen as a gift. Not so much like a much hoped for, gift wrapped, birthday present. More like a wake-up call to get you to rise up and do something radically different in your life. Change occurs much more frequently when we are hurting than when we are comfortably sitting knee deep in our own status quo.

I received my gift at an early age being a child of the holocaust of World War II. I distinctly remember being told about the horrors that my mother, Valeria, experienced escaping from German Gestapo patrols for the final two years of the war. In a heroic attempt to avoid capture and almost certain deportation to a concentration camp, she and her first husband and two children fled to the forests of Slovakia, leaving behind every possession that they couldn't carry on their backs. Anything that was left behind was looted by the Germans when they overran Czechoslovakia.

Tragically one day, her husband and two children were captured by German patrols, lined up against a wall with 125 other "innocents," machine gunned to death and then unceremoniously thrown into an open pit. Unfortunately, that was only part of the "unimaginable human conduct" that she experienced over the next few years

She survived by eating potato peels and other bits of discarded food that she scavenged daily from trash dumps, garbage cans and the forest floor. The two winters she endured were particularly harsh, and she endured frostbite and near hypothermia for months at a time.

When she begged for assistance from the very people that she had previously employed when she was a factory owner, she was consistently turned away empty handed.

After the war, she exhumed the bodies of her husband and 2 children from the mass grave, identified them by their clothing and arranged for their burial in individual graves in the Jewish tradition.

Unbelievably, she lost any new possessions she had, when the Soviets froze the assets of anyone who sought to escape Communist rule after they invaded Czechoslovakia at the end of the war.

That's a slice of life that no human being should ever have to experience. Her holocaust experience was horrific. Many other people in other countries all over the world have also undergone their own "personal holocaust," with equally unimaginable experiences. Consider grandparents who were enslaved in the United States prior to the Civil War, parents and grandparents who were locked up in Japanese internment camps in the United States during the war, and parents and grandparents who endured great hardships and suffering during the Great Depression of the 1930's.

Many individuals have endured great pain and suffering from illness, as victims of crime, abuse, discrimination. Others have witnessed or participated in war-related atrocities. Many others live in poverty, hunger, and suffering or have been victims of natural disasters. Clearly, no list can be complete as each day reveals other holocausts and tragedies around the world.

The issue is not *how many* people encounter and feel hurt. That is one of the "givens" of the human condition. It is what they do following exposure to unimaginable or deep hurt that counts. The issue is *how resilient* they are.

In his seminal work, "Man's Search for Meaning," Viktor Frankl noted that there were at least 2 types of people who emerged from the concentration camps after WWII. One group was essentially physically, spiritually and emotionally devastated. What they had experienced shook the very core and foundation of their beliefs about humanity. Many of these people became isolated and lived silently in the shadows, alleys and back streets of their communities. Many of these people refused to discuss what had happened to them and their families and friends.

Others were fearful to speak up for many reasons during their entire lifetimes. This was due to fears (realistic and unrealistic) that new tragedies would befall them. My father (who my mother met and married following the war) was such a man. His advice to me during childhood largely consisted of telling me to cause no undue attention to come my way. This advice came from a combination of fatherly protectiveness and a profound paranoia that the Soviets would overrun the USA in due time as they had Hungary, Czechoslovakia and much of Eastern Europe in the 1940's and 1950's.

The other group of survivors, whose reactions were significantly different from people like my father, described by Frankl found a way to sustain hope on a daily basis throughout their ordeal. Some did that by imagining foods they might eat if they survived. Others dreamed of joyous reunions with loved ones who had become separated from them during the war. Frankl describes how he sought to bring joy to others by offering a piece of his daily bread ration or by offering a simple smile. Just wishing someone "Good Sabbath" was a way of rekindling faith and hope that one day there might be a "Good Sabbath" again. It was not the magnitude of the gesture that mattered as much as the heart felt sincerity attached to it. In their dreadful environment of inhumanity, any spark of decency could kindle the flickering flame of hope.

After the war, these people often became bold, outspoken champions of the downtrodden. They swore that "Never Again" would they stand by and watch the merciless slaughter of innocents. Their voices would ring out at every opportunity, regardless of personal cost and consequences.

. . What is the essential difference between these two groups of people? How could the same deep and unimaginable hurt devastate some yet invigorate others? The answer is comparatively easy to describe, although immeasurably harder to do. One of the critical elements is how the deep hurt that they endured was experienced, interpreted and ultimately "reframed." Those people who could understand and accept the hurt as being meaningful to them reframed it to serve as an inspiration and motivation to move forward. Those who could not understand why this had happened to them and reframe the experience put up personal, psychological and emotional walls in a desperate attempt to prevent such hurt from ever affecting them.

In my life, I came to a serious crossroads shortly after my 13th birthday. I had been born in Czechoslovakia in 1948. My family came to the United States in 1949, when I was a year old, to live permanently. All of our first names were changed so that we would be able to assimilate and blend in within our new community in New York City. As I noted just above, I had constantly been told to "blend in and not stand out." Given what my parents had been through, they considered this to be a prudent life suggestion.

I didn't speak English until I was 5 years old and was very awkward and shy in school. I did not have a lot of friends and always felt like somewhat of an outsider. While other kids went to parties and socialized regularly with one another, I was usually the kid on the outside, looking in. Needless to say, this caused me a lot of personal pain. Life did not look easy or much FUN at this point.

I still resonate today to outsiders. I consider myself a "magnet for the odd." If there are 100 people in a room, and one odd person walks in, they will usually gravitate to me. Why? Because the other 99 people will do their level best to avert this person's gaze, while I will make eye contact. I relate to odd people because I was (and still am to some degree) one.

Shortly after I turned 13, I remember telling my dad that "not only was I never going to blend in again, but that I was going to stand up and stand out." If there was trouble coming my way, I was going to face it and deal with it head on. I was determined to be noticed. I would not go quietly into the night.

I will never forget the horrified look on my dad's face. He felt that I was abandoning a more prudent path for an unknown journey that was sure to cause me great difficulty.

I had no plan. No support from anyone. Just a fantasy image in my mind of a character who was basically "unassaultable." A character who could stand up in any situation and speak his mind. A character who would have to be reckoned with. To avoid the constant pain of seeing myself as awkward, I was determined to become this character. Ironically, this would become my persona on stage as a speaker 30 years later. No one ever said it would be easy or in my case, FAST. But you know what? The pain and awkwardness is gone.

First, I started to read psychology books. I thought that this would allow me to understand what other people were thinking. I also learned to play guitar, forced myself to speak in public, and attempted to tell jokes whenever and wherever I could. If an opportunity presented itself to stand up and stand out, I took it. I failed more often than I succeeded, BUT I kept my eyes on the prize, knowing that reverting back to being a socially introverted, awkward and uncomfortable teen was less palatable.

In reality, there was going to be pain either way I looked at it. I already knew the pain I had suffered when I was awkward and introverted. The pain of failing to be funny or failing to draw attention to myself in a more positive way seemed slight by comparison. It is all about the figure and the background. How I chose to see the different types of pain that were available determined what I was willing to risk.

My first attempts at performing comedy on stage are also worth mentioning here. Today, I currently work as a stand-up comic and humorous business speaker. I went to audition on Amateur Night at a local comedy club In San Diego, California. I invited well over 100 people to my debut. I was certain that my debut would be hailed as legendary. I had visions of being catapulted into comedy stardom immediately following the show.

Sadly, this was not how it turned out. On amateur nights, the audience views itself like the spectators at the Roman Coliseum in its heyday. They either want the comedic gladiators to be very funny or to die a horrible, agonizing death and never return. The audience got what they wanted as I died a horrible comedic death. The only laugh I got was when I deadpanned to the audience that "I didn't do this for a living." That was painfully clear to the audience. At the end of the show, friends weren't sure whether I had exhibited courage or brain damage. Nevertheless, I was determined to return.

Weeks of rehearsal and numerous episodes of panic stricken vomiting led to three more consecutive, disastrous comedic failures. At times, I was left wondering whether I could ever really be "funny for money." Four times I had attempted to be funny and four times I had not only failed but had been completely humiliated as well. I'd like to say here that "what doesn't kill you only makes you stronger," but I certainly didn't feel that way, nor did the comedy club owner when I showed up for a 5th time.

When he saw my name on the list of would be performers, he came over to me and said, "Look, you're just not very funny." I remember my final plea to let me try one more time. I told him, "Each of the four previous times, I kept trying to please the audience. I had never allowed myself to have FUN on stage, just being me. This one time, I just wanted to enjoy myself on stage and have FUN. The heck with the audience. I just wanted to play. Me, Mr. Microphone and the stage were all that mattered on that night. And if that wasn't FUNNY enough for the audience, I will never darken your door again."

He looked at me with a combination of pity and intrigue and said, "What the heck. I'll put you on after 11:00 PM." This was not a favorable slot as the audience could be quite rowdy by this point, having consumed alcohol non-stop for over 2 hours. They wouldn't have much patience or tolerance. At a comedy club, the rule of thumb is that you had better make the audience laugh every 20-30 seconds if you want to survive your time.

When my turn came up, I went to the stage, grabbed the microphone and just started to chat with the audience. Audiences don't laugh gratuitously. You have to make them laugh. To get an audience to laugh, you have to do several things:

1) Be real. Tell the truth in a funny way.
2) Have a comedic character that fits you and your material. If only someone had told me this before my first attempt, I could have spared myself a lot of heartache and humiliation.
3) Touch the audience's heart by getting them to like you.
4) Get off stage on a high note before they get tired of you or figure you out.

On that night, everything clicked. I just told them how I felt about things in the world. Even in their alcoholic stupor, they related. More importantly, they laughed. A lot. My five minutes flew by, and I left the stage to the applause that I had been craving.

I went home and danced in the dark for 3 hours, alone. I had triumphed. All of the pain and suffering had been worth it.

And that is the key point.

When you finally overcome an obstacle and succeed, there are few feelings in the world that are more powerful. Success is a great drug. It instills confidence like nothing else can.

I didn't become a professional comic right away, but I was addicted to the applause and laughter. There were other missteps along the way, but no amount of pain or fear could keep me from trying to be "funny for money." That's what anyone needs to get started. One success that you are proud of. I will never forget the pride I felt the first time I was truly funny on a stage.

Other people can create a sense of urgency based on a single experience. Consider Enrique.

ENRIQUE

During the 1980's I was invited to work with DEA agents in Central America. The story of one agent who was stationed in Guatemala is particularly relevant here. Enrique was DEA's sole representative in Guatemala. He was not attached to the embassy and had no ability to arrest anyone, yet he fancied himself to be a one-man, drug-busting squad.

Enrique had spent 5 years undercover attempting to set up a heroin dealer to take a fall. At great personal cost and risk, he had infiltrated the dealer's drug cartel. His long and hard work finally resulted in the capture of this individual, who was extradited to the US to stand trial. Bail was set at $20 million dollars, which was delivered to the court in cash within hours of the hearing. The man was released, and I am sure left the country by private jet within hours. Enrique received a phone call on his private line within 24 hours from this dealer, who told him, "I am back and you are a dead man." Enrique left the country temporarily and was reassigned but continued to work undercover during a long and illustrious career.

When I spoke to Enrique, I asked him why he continued to pursue his very dangerous career. He recounted a very moving story. He said that, during his first year at DEA, he had gone into a public bathroom and found a young 15-year-old girl dead on the floor from a heroin overdose. The hypodermic needle that carried her fatal dose was lying on the floor right next to her body. He took the needle, put it in his bag and thought about his own 15-year-old daughter and how distraught he would be if something like that ever happened to her. He swore to himself that, regardless of the cost, he would find the dealer who sold drugs to this girl and stop him from doing it to someone else. It took a long time, but he eventually made good on his promise and continued to work in the field for over 20 years. Whenever his work became frightening or challenging, he just flashed on the sight of the original victim DOA on the bathroom floor.

FINDING YOUR PURPOSE

For some of us, it just takes one seminal event to change our lives and give us a grounded sense of meaning and purpose. One sentence said at the right time by the right person in the right way or one significant experience can change another person's life forever. We have each been given a gift to use during our lifetime. You may have understood your gift early in life. Maybe you will grasp it later in life. If you haven't realized your gift just yet, hopefully, you will at least spend some time seeking to know it soon.

I know that once people come to terms with what their "mission on earth is," they find it easier to overcome pain and obstacles in order to "get on with their mission." Your job is no longer "just a job." Now it can become a "calling."

What is the difference? It is all about the way in which you interpret the meaning that it has for you. Doing meaningful things becomes more important than allowing yourself to get sidetracked with hurt and other issues.

Not every problem relates to core issues. However, energy diverted to dealing with past hurts prevents you from bringing full energy and intensity to bear towards whatever you choose to do during your life. Imagine the energy and intensity that you could have if the energy wasted on small problems such as overeating, excessing shopping, or being neat freak could all be redirected in a more focused manner.

Rising up from your hurt can help you to do just that.

Chapter 10

WHAT IF I AM STUCK?

NANCY

Nancy weighed close to 250 pounds and tried every new diet that she heard about. She tried fasts, liquid diets, diet pills and unusual combinations of foods (such as the cabbage diet.) Like many people, Nancy typically lost and then gained a few pounds at some point during her diet. This yoyo-like behavior was very frustrating to her and led to the abandonment of each diet (usually within 3 weeks), followed by the futile search for a "new and better diet," a few months later.

Does this sound familiar? It doesn't really matter what diet you are on. The same general process will occur. The first week of your diet (assuming that you actually ate less food), you lost 2 pounds. Your body hadn't figured out what you were doing yet, so it gave up a little weight. By the second week of your diet, your body, which now had deduced that you were, in fact, consuming less food, changed your metabolic rate (the rate at which you burn calories). Unless you were willing to dramatically increase your exercise rate (by doubling it, at least), you didn't lose much, if any, weight during the second week of the diet. By the third week of the diet, food was now attacking your body. You were walking around with a sausage coming out of your mouth, and you really had no idea how it got there.

Most diets result in "binges" shortly after the third week, thus returning you to your original weight (give or take a few pounds.) You go on these binges because you have felt deprived during the diet AND you hadn't lost the weight you wanted. Might as well eat and enjoy then.

People, like Nancy, get STUCK on the diet/binge merry-go-round because they are unwilling to look carefully at the payoffs/benefits that they derive from eating.

If you weigh too much, let's consider WHEN you eat too much. Sadly, most people do not consume just the foods that they like. Most people, in fact, don't even really get much of a taste sensation at all from some of the food they consume. If you eat an entire bag of HoHos, you will register 2 strong taste sensations. The first taste sensation of immense pleasure will come from the first few bites. You will be amazed at how good the snack is. You will swear that this food is the "nectar of the gods."

However, the more you eat, the less you will taste. Remember that you are not eating these HoHos because you are hungry. Most of the time you are eating this after dinner or for an in-between meal snack.

The second and last taste sensation you experience will come from the last microscopic morsel that you scoop out from the bottom of the bag with your pinky. This will be accompanied by the sad realization that you have now consumed the entire bag of HoHos. If you are really sad, you may actually get up to see if there is another bag of HoHos in the house.

So why do people do this? Night after night? Day after day? What are the payoffs/benefits for this seemingly counterproductive behavior?

The answer has little to do with the actual food. Forget the food. Let's look at how Nancy feels just prior to eating. If you ask Nancy, she says she feels a bit restless, nervous or maybe even anxious. Rather than dealing with how she is feeling and CAREfronting herself, she finds herself drawn to eating her favorite comfort foods like HoHos.

Most people eat too much when they don't feel good about themselves, their situation or life in general. Here is what it comes down to in the simplest of terms.

Nancy can face her feelings, deal with them and search for options to change/accept her feelings of hurt

OR

She can do something else that will temporarily distract her from those feelings.

She can face the fact that she is not happy about something in her life (related to her weight)

OR

She can inhale those HoHos.

There are two types of choices. Which is easier? Active CAREfrontation with yourself and how you feel OR immediate self-gratification? Nancy should not be surprised when she is cleaning those crumbs off of her blouse at how easy it had been for her to make that decision without really ever thinking about it.

That's how hidden and unconscious payoffs/benefits work. If you want to lose weight, you must first recognize the possible payoffs/benefits for NOT losing weight such as:

1) Whenever you are not happy, you can get happy (at least for a short while) by eating something like that entire bag of HoHos.

2) Whenever you think about how much you weigh, you have a good reason not to exercise because it just takes too much effort, and it will take so long to lose any real weight. After all, you have had a big belly/butt/thigh since you were 30. Maybe a few HoHos would taste really good right now.

3) Since you have lost weight before, only to regain it all again, why should you have to experience that sense of failure and frustration again when you could just have a HoHo?

4) You choose to judge yourself based on your "good intentions" to lose weight rather than on your outcomes/impacts where you don't keep the weight off for long. You deserve to be rewarded for your good intentions. So you eat a HoHo.

5) Since other people may not find you appealing, why should you work at it? They are just shallow anyway, and after all isn't that Hoho your only "TRUE FRIEND?"

6) Friends don't always love you, but HoHos do.

It is so seductive to accept the easy and quick answer. We have created a society where bad feelings can be quickly and immediately erased by food, drink, cigarettes, medicine, sex, gambling, drugs, video games or a thousand other paths. Actually dealing with those feelings just takes too long, can hurt and offers us no guarantee that you will feel better anyway. The heck with it.

At the moment, the choice feels right. The problem isn't really that bad. It isn't going to get worse by tomorrow, so you'll get to deal with it then. Days become weeks. Weeks become months. Months turn into years. Years turn into lifetimes. Haven't YOU been STUCK for TOO LONG? Choosing to escape from tough feelings by some temporary escape route is SHORT-TERM Smart but LONG-TERM Not So Smart.

Of course, facing the real issue, which has little to do with eating, is much deeper than that. We will visit with Nancy again in Chapter 15, when we discuss "reframing" the issue.

TEDDY

Here is another example:

Teddy was a nail biter and a cuticle picker. He usually covered his hands or kept them out of sight on dates and business meetings. He used Band-Aids and foul tasting cream that he dabbed on his fingers (to avoid biting them) to no avail. He had no need for a manicure because he didn't have finger nails. He even had to go to his doctor for medications when his fingers became infected from his constant attention.

What are the payoff/benefits for this behavior? No one really wants to see their fingers bloody or bleeding all of the time, do they?

Again, if we just look at the behavior and ignore how Teddy was feeling prior to the behavior, we miss the point. Teddy did not like to be late. But guess what? He was regularly late to most of his appointments, dates, meetings and movies. Like most "lateniks," he was always just trying to get one more thing done before he left his house or office.

So now Teddy was driving down the road at 20 miles faster than the speed limit. His car was almost going sideways, as he maneuvered from lane to lane, trying to find the fastest way to "get there." Inevitably, he glanced down at one of his hands and saw a tiny piece of skin that was "out of place." At this point, he felt compelled to "groom." "Grooming" consisted of taking skin that was currently on his fingers and RIPPING IT OFF his fingers. Followed in close order by bleeding. Followed by a variety of behaviors to stem the bleeding.

This included putting his finger into his mouth and sucking the blood off the finger. If a tissue was handy, it included dabbing his finger with a

Kleenex. It included squeezing the finger, followed by sucking and/or more dabbing. At some point, mercifully, the blood stopped flowing. If Teddy was really late, he saw another piece of skin out of place and started the process all over again.

So why did Teddy do this? Night after night? Day after day? What were the payoffs/benefits for this seemingly counterproductive, self-destructive behavior?

The answer had little to do with Teddy's fingers or blood. Forget the blood. Look at how Teddy felt just prior to picking at his fingers. If you asked Teddy, he said he was just trying to get to his destination. But deeper down, he was more concerned about having to provide yet another lame excuse to justify his tardiness. He hated the thought of having to explain, yet again, why he was not able to "get there" on time. Rather than dealing with how he was feeling and CAREfronting himself, he found himself drawn to distracting himself by picking at his fingers.

People pick at their cuticles and/or bite their nails when they don't feel good about themselves, their situation or in Teddy's case—being late again. Here is what it comes down to in the simplest of terms.

Teddy can face his feelings and guilt about always being late, deal with them and search for options to change/accept his feelings of hurt

OR

He can do something else that will temporarily distract him from those feelings.

Which is EASIER?

He can face the fact that he continues to be late and has to make excuses all of the time

OR

He can pick at his fingers.

Again, don't be surprised when Teddy is sucking on his finger at how easy it was for him to make that decision without ever really thinking about it.

Of course, facing the real issue, which has little to do with lateness, nail biting or cuticle picking is much deeper than that. We will visit with Teddy again in Chapter 15 when we discuss "reframing" the issue.

Forget about Nancy and Teddy. Why are YOU STUCK? What payoffs do you have for keeping YOUR hurt? Think of the benefits that you derive for doing what on the surface may look like a counterproductive behavior.

When you allow yourself to get stuck, you usually are:

1) not owning the payoffs for your issue
2) not willing to consider the issue from different and possibly deeper levels
3) not dealing with the "potential pain and fear" of making a change in a positive manner
4) not clear on what options are available to you
   OR
5) not in enough pain to motivate you to make a change.

Let's look at some ways to get unstuck.

Chapter 11

GETTING "UNSTUCK"

Two of the most frustrating problems that occur when we consider ourselves to be "STUCK" are:

1) You can't think of any options
   OR
2) You have found a few options, but all you can see is how difficult it would be to implement them.

Your goal should always be to find at least 3 ways to view your issue and at least 3 options to rise up from your hurt.

If you don't know what to do when you get "STUCK," your mind may start to engage in counterproductive behaviors such as:

1) shutting down
2) distracting yourself with other thoughts
3) thinking only about the same options you have already tried
4) getting angry or frustrated with the person that brought up the issue
5) getting angry or frustrated with yourself and your lack of ability to find options
6) thinking you are "stupid"
7) thinking that the issue is "stupid"
8) giving up and accepting the idea that THERE ARE NO OPTIONS or only BAD OPTIONS.

People who can readily see options rarely get STUCK because they have tactics to help them shift their perspective on the issue and possible options to solve the issue.

So what should you do?

Here are 10 tactics that can help you get "UNSTUCK":

1) Randomly recombine previously successful options. In simpler terms, go back and see what worked before to see if you can tweak your past successes to find a new option. Build on your past successes. Before you seek "new" answers, review your past and see if some of the answers that worked before can be modified, altered, updated or simplified to yield a new option. You have faced many problems in the past and solved many of them quite successfully. What did it take then? What will it take now?

2) Ask yourself what definitions, rules and assumptions you are making about the current problem. Many times you can't see options because of the way in which you define the issue. Sometimes, you continue to use rules or guidelines that made sense previously when dealing with other problems. They may have been appropriate at another time. Are they still viable? Are they still current? Do they still fit the situation? As a child, you may have been told to sit quietly and say nothing when in the company of others. That may have made sense when you were five. Does it still make sense at forty-five?

3) Look for the most obvious answers. Sometimes, they are so obvious that they are overlooked. They may be staring you right between the eyes, but your perspective may be on the horizon. See the problem from the "boots on the ground" perspective. Then get up to the 1,000 foot level and see what it looks like. Does it look any different from the 10,000 foot level? You bet it does.

Look at any FedEx logo on a truck, lock box or envelope. There is a symbol hidden in that logo. Some people have no idea of what the hidden symbol is. It is an arrow. Some people can't see the arrow. Why not? Because they are too busy looking at the letters. Try looking at the white space between the letters. Try looking at the white space between the last E and X. See the arrow now? Once you can find the arrow, see if you can find the hidden spoon. It is in the white space inside the first E.

The difference between being stuck and getting "unstuck" may be as simple as the vantage point you take to view the problem or the options.

4) Ask someone else. This sounds so simple, but so many cultures frown on people admitting that they are stuck let alone letting someone else know that they are stuck. You may perceive asking questions or admitting that you are stuck as a sign of weakness, inadequacy or stupidity. Just the

opposite is true. The mark of a courageous person is the ability to ask the right questions of the right people at the right time. The more questions asked, the more chances you have to uncover options that you may have overlooked.

5) Brainstorm with several other people. The more the merrier. Generate a reasonable quantity of options. Don't worry about the quality of the options until you are further along in the process. Brainstorming with others can extend the parameters to choose options. At 3M, they used to give an award for the "worst suggestion offered" periodically. They have a culture that truly comprehends the notion that all suggestions have value. The real value may not be the suggestion itself. It may be that it stimulates you to think differently and find new options.

6) Restate the problem using an analogy. When our egos are at stake in the issue, psychological defenses can quickly creep in and may preclude our ability to see options that are perceived as unsettling. To avoid this, find an impersonal analogy to the problem that will allow your mind to face virtually the same issue without the ego involvement. This derives from a notion used at Harvard called "Synectics" or problem solving by analogy. It allows "bright outsiders" who have little knowledge of the actual problem to participate by having them work on the analogy only. Sometimes the options used to solve the analogy can transfer directly to the initial problem.

7) Do some "Blue Sky" thinking. Forget about the issue or starting point, and just look at interesting options. You can always work in reverse order to get back to the issue. You may feel compelled to start with the problem as given and proceed in a linear fashion from there. Remember an issue can be viewed from any perspective. Why should you always view it from the start? Why not start in the middle? Or at the end? Just because you don't start at the beginning doesn't mean you can't work your way back there.

8) Call a Time Out. Get your mind onto something else for a little while and then return to the issue. Naps work well here. Puzzles work well here too. While you are resting or dealing with another issue, your mind may still be processing the initial issue. The danger here is that you may get fully absorbed in the new activity and find it much easier or more fun to deal with. You may find it hard to return to the ultimate issue. However,

options do not come at a steady, consistent rate, and persistence is what pays off in the long run.

9) Play the "What If" game. Sometimes if we alter the limits, parameters or constraints on the original issue, new options spontaneously emerge. Often, a nuanced variation can totally reframe our perspective. Changing the time perspective from a Short-Term View to a Long-Term View could be significant or vice versa. Just opening up your mind to inquiry can clear the logjam.

10) Believe in your own ability and have faith in yourself. This is a time for PMA (Positive Mental Attitude). The main value of PMA is to avoid NMA (Negative Mental Attitude). Your brain works in a significantly different manner when you start to become negative or depressed. Once you begin to feel defeated, older more primitive sectors of the brain can influence what you are thinking in a more dramatic fashion. Remember that fear and pain can be huge influencers in your ability and willingness to face issues.

You begin to react with the fight-flight impulse of getting away from the issue because you deem it potentially painful. You must believe down deep that you can survive (or even possibly thrive through) the problem. Resilient people know that they will find a way.

Chapter 12

HOW TO DECIDE WHICH OPTION IS RIGHT FOR YOU

In Chapter 4, we took a look at SELF CONCEPT and its importance in your ability to address your pain. Before you can start rising up from your hurt, you will have to find a way to evaluate your options. It is important to do this based on your SELF CONCEPT so that the option(s) you select feel(s) right to you. Using criteria that are general or do not fit you will backfire and sabotage your ability to rise up from your hurt.

Think of what is important to your SELF CONCEPT *before* you select Options so that you will more confident in the options you choose.

Other factors to consider when evaluating options are listed below.

1)   EASE OF IMPLEMENTATION

Many self-help books will tell you that all your problems will be solved if only you do X. They make it sound easy. After all, isn't that we all would like? An easy fix to a complicated problem? While it is important to go after the "low hanging fruit" FIRST in order to get some traction with your issue, bear in mind that these first steps are only a scratch on the surface of where we need to go. However, it is these first steps that we will use to help get you started. Success breeds success. The earlier you make some progress, the better. Keep in mind, however, that once initial changes are made, the road will get more difficult and challenging. Trust that this is par for the course. And it is this road, the tougher and longer road, that you must give consideration to so that you have set up realistic expectations for the journey ahead.

The typical course for rising up from your hurt looks like this:

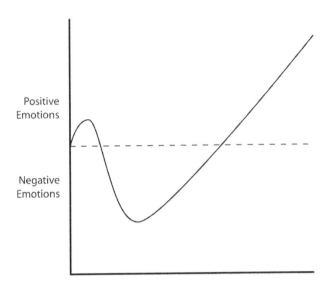

Once you mentally commit to an option but don't actually have to do anything yet, you allow yourself to become excited about the possibilities. You begin to imagine life without an anchor around your neck. It is much like the overweight person who believes that they will start their diet TOMORROW. This allows them to freely eat today and suffer no pain, since the "FIX" is in place starting the next day. This is fine since it acts like THE UNBALANCED FORCE to get you started. It starts the body in motion.

However, once you begin to really CAREFRONT your deeper feelings and the various definitions of the issue, you may begin to understand that it may not be as simple as you had hoped. As this reality sets in and you see the road ahead, hopefully you will accept the notion that the road may become more difficult before it becomes easier.

As you fully evaluate your payoffs and your pain threshold, you must accept the fact that it will not take 1 day to "dig yourself out of a hole" that you have spent 10 years or more digging yourself into. You must welcome the descent into thoughts and feelings that may have lay submerged and unquestioned for many years. Feeling feelings that have been under the surface for many years is not an easy process.

Too often, the therapeutic "50-minute hour" does not serve us well during this period of time. Typically, a therapist will spend the first 10-15 minutes regaining rapport with a client by either catching up on what has transpired since the last session or reviewing what they discussed during the previous session. Assuming that there are "no games" being played by the client (which is a big assumption when the client is on the cusp of real CAREFRONTATION with their issues), the therapist and client then gingerly move ahead.

Since most therapists don't want to open up cans of worms that they can't help their client digest, they must begin to wind the session down with 10-15 minutes to go so that the client can leave "emotionally intact" as opposed to "emotionally distraught." That leaves 20-30 minutes of real work time when progress can be made. When a client gets upset, as they are likely to do amidst CAREFRONTATION, it is vitally important to deal actively with those emerging feelings with acceptance and forgiveness.

Resist the temptation to reach for a box of tissues or to accept those offered to you. Tissues can be used as subtle signs to get you to stop feeling bad and not get your clothes messed up. Purging your soul is far more important than keeping your clothes clean. Rising up from your hurt demands that you "feel what you need to feel." That is sometimes hard to do within the "50-minute hour" framework.

At certain points in the process, rising up from your hurt requires longer blocks of time to break through to the "core" issues. If you know you are headed towards an emotionally dark space, you may choose to go in the express lane or in the local lane. The choice is yours. The choice is made as a function of the type of pain you prefer to deal with. When you need to pull a Band-Aid off, do your prefer to rip it off quickly and feel the pain all at once or slowly peel it off minimizing the amount of pain that you feel at any point, but prolonging the total amount of time that you are in pain?

At some point along the way, you may hit "rock bottom." You will see who you are at your core; accept that and begin to see the light ahead more clearly. This means that you can start the upward climb towards living without this issue. The pace of change can increase dramatically at this point now knowing that you have survived the descent into what you had previously perceived as insurmountable pain. Knowing that it did not kill or cripple you may motivate you to move more briskly.

As long as you keep your eyes on the prize, which is filled with freedom and possibility, you can endure the discomfort of change and continue to put one foot in front of the other and march onward.

Hopefully, you now realistically see what it will take for you to rise up from your hurt and accelerate the process. Early successes and easy first steps may a good way to use to start the process. However, if you continue to use ease as a criteria later in the process, you may abandon or slow down your ability to rise up from your hurt.

2) COST/EFFORT REQUIRED TO IMPLEMENT SOLUTION

Potential costs to consider may include financial cost, emotional cost, and physical cost. Depending on the issue, you might be able to conduct a simple cost benefit analysis to determine whether or not rising up from your hurt is worth it.

For instance, if you are going to stop smoking, you could compare the cost of using the nicotine patch or going to a hypnotist to the cost of continuing to smoke a pack a day. In the long run, you may also want to factor in the potential health care costs of long-term smoking. However, don't let cost be the sole criteria that you use.

In the case of smoking, dealing with the nicotine addiction, the physical cravings from withdrawal and doing without cigarettes during tough or pleasant times may clearly outweigh the financial issues when it comes to deciding whether or not you really want to stop.

Physical cost may also be important, particularly when it comes to reshaping our bodies through exercise. Think of how many New Year's resolutions you have written about taking that daily walk/run or bike ride. You swore that you would be willing to get up at 6:00 AM three days a week and walk/run for 20 minutes. It seemed like such a reasonable goal on December 29, when you wrote it down. You may even have done it for a week or two in January, feeling energized by the brisk cool air. You were rightfully proud of the fact that you had stuck to your guns, got up when you didn't want to and braved the cold and the darkness.

Then January 15th rolled around, and it was raining at 6:00 AM, and you didn't sleep that well the night before. No problem. You passed on walking that morning, swearing that you would do it the next day. And then… (you can fill it the good reason/excuse that you used.) A few days became a week. One week turned into 2 weeks, and by then the resolution was a distant memory.

When you use physical cost as a decision factor, you have to learn to welcome pain and discomfort as your friend and ally. That may involve a redefinition of how you deal with pain and discomfort. Coping with your pain becomes a sign of your persistence and commitment. Discomfort becomes a "badge of honor" to wear proudly.

This learning is necessary to rise up from your hurt because it is a clear demonstration that the pain you only imagined was not the actual pain you experienced. Your imagination viewed the pain as unbearable and intolerable, and, while getting up from a poor night's sleep and launching yourself into the freezing cold for a quick walk isn't easy, once you've done it, you can celebrate your success of moving yourself one day further into your resolution. Your experience has now showed you that you could overcome the pain without collapsing. That lesson alone is worth its weight in gold.

Financial or physical costs can be "tangible," easily measured factors in some cases. However, don't let the lure of easy measurement outweigh other less tangible, but potentially more meaningful, emotional factors. Emotional costs, though harder to measure, are more likely to be a critical factor in reaching your success.

Consider Jimmy's situation.

JIMMY

Jimmy always felt that he was under pressure to live up the expectations of other people. It started off with just trying to please his father. Next, it extended to pleasing his teachers. Then it was his boss. Then it extended to almost everyone around him. Everyone always expected Jimmy to be "the most likely to succeed." Anything less than an "A" in school was considered a failure for Jimmy. Not getting a promotion was considered a failure. Not winning every game of basketball was considered a failure.

Jimmy's entire definition of success was based on being the best. But it was killing him inside.

For Jimmy, the emotional cost of changing his definition of success meant having to face his father and other key figures in his life to tell them that he was tired of having to compete constantly with the world around him. He was tired of living by the maxim that "Winning wasn't everything. Winning was the ONLY THING."

Just one time, he wanted to play for the sheer joy of playing. The score wouldn't matter. He dreaded seeing the look of scorn that he was sure his father, his boss or his pals would have on their faces. He didn't want to hear harsh words describing how he had "let his old man or the company or his team down."

But that might be part of Jimmy's price for emotional freedom. Being upfront with how he feels (or thinks he may feel) will allow him to redefine success for himself in a way that matched his SELF CONCEPT. At that point, he could then be able to give himself permission to enjoy the journey without total commitment and focus on the result.

Emotional costs, particularly when coupled with anticipated, exaggerated, unknown pain, have stopped many people from rising up from their hurt. Will you allow it stop you?

There are many people like Jimmy who are unwilling to tell Dad or another important life figure how they really felt while they are alive. Sharing those feelings with a headstone after they have passed on may seem easier on the surface, but it doesn't feel as good in the long run. It also doesn't make up for years of having to absorb pain from doing things that did not fit your SELF CONCEPT.

Emotional criteria are so critical that they are usually part of every successful plan to rise up from your hurt. Few other criteria are as intricately involved with changing your life.

3) TIME NEEDED TO IMPLEMENT SOLUTION

This factor addresses the issues of sense of urgency and how fast you want to change. I believe that speed really matters. Life is short. Every day spent hurting is a day gone forever. You can never reclaim it. There are no do-overs.

I am in a rush. I am impatient. I believe you should be as well with whatever ails you. However, I can't force you to move at a faster speed when you are more comfortable at a slower pace.

Some of you are Type "A", multi-taskers, adrenaline junkies and boredom-phobics. For you, almost no speed or amount of overstimulation is overwhelming. The more the better. If one is good, two should be twice as good.

Others are more Type "B" serial problem solvers, even-keeled and cautious when encountering change. For you, better safe than sorry is much more comfortable. Less may be more. And if one is good, let's finish that one before we go on to another.

The critical variable here then is not only speed, but your perceptions of the issue, options and the probabilities of success. Just deciding whether or not to use this factor will tell you a lot about how you see the issue.

There is a new brand of science entitled Chaos Theory. An interesting phrase was coined by chaos theorists. It was the term "chaorder," a combination of the word chaos and the word order. In describing how a person would feel about quick change, here is what the theorists said.

It doesn't matter how fast the world (your issue) is moving, it only matters how fast you are moving in relationship to it. If you are moving more slowly than the problem, everything else will seem to be moving very fast and appear to be random. This could certainly cause you to become fearful and slow down even further. However, if you are moving faster than the issue, it will appear to slow down and everything will appear to be more orderly and predictable. That alone should provide a reasonable rationale for faster movement.

However, you can't move faster than your comfort zone allows.

I invite you to expand your comfort zone, minimize your perception of future pain, be optimistic and hopeful about options and long-term success and your rate of speed may increase.

While there is no such thing as the "right speed" in general for rising up from hurt, there is a "right speed" for you. Take a look back at how fast you have worked on other problems in your life. What you may find is that you were willing to work faster when you saw more options to solve the issue and were more optimistic about your overall success.

4) SHORT TERM vs. LONG TERM PERSPECTIVE

If you hurt right now, you may initially feel more comfortable with options that immediately reduce the current level of hurt. That is the grand allure of fast acting medication, one more drink, cigarette, or food. In the short run, you choose to ignore what lies underneath the surface in service of reducing immediate hurt. Once the immediate hurt is gone, you may even believe that the problem is solved. And it is. For a short while.

DENISE

Denise is frightened of being stuck in elevators and other confined spaces. However, she can be taught how to meditate, breathe more deeply or use a hypnotic suggestion to relieve the immediate fear of the elevator. She may be offered a medication that will "calm her nerves" so that when she gets into an elevator, the panic will be reduced. Behavioral therapists believe that the errant behavior "is the problem." Once the behavior is eliminated, the problem is then considered solved. In the short run, it may in fact seem solved.

However, since Denise never inquired about the payoffs for having a fear of elevators and never investigated whether or not that feeling was the real issue or a symptom of a more far reaching issue, it would not be surprising to find Denise fearful about having an MRI, making a phone call in a phone booth or standing in the middle of a crowded bus. This is one of the common issues that surfaces when clients are treated with only with short-term behavior modification therapy.

The same issue may manifest itself in another related form because Denise did not go more deeply into the issue. She was willing to accept short-term reduction of panic as sufficient. She was so happy not to be concerned about elevators again that she never considered that other small confining spaces might trigger the identical panic reaction at a future time.

Taking the long-term view of the issue might involve Denise looking back over her entire life for events that caused similar panic reactions. Potentially, it might reveal the triggering events that set the panic attacks in motion in the first place.

Is it scary to look deep into the soul for memories that may be frightening? Yes it is. Is there any guarantee that looking for trigger events will yield them? Of course not. Many of those thoughts have been hidden from conscious thought for long periods of time. The memories of those events can be so frightening or terrifying that putting them out of her mind made for easier "closure" than remembering them.

Remember Denise wants "peace of mind" and can conveniently "forget" things that would disrupt that "peace of mind." The memories aren't gone. The memory traces have been made. They are just hard to retrieve.

Since Denise lived in a small town where there weren't many buildings over three stories tall, she just avoided elevators, convincing herself that it was "healthier" to walk up and down the flights of stairs rather than take the elevator. Trips to big cities were few and far between, so the panic of being in an elevator was only a minor disruption in her life.

Think of your issue. Are you more interested in ridding yourself of temporary pain, or do you want to eliminate the issue once and for all? Many people make decisions which are short-term smart, but long term not so smart, because they don't think about the role the problem has played during the course of their entire lives. How about you?

5) PAIN THRESHHOLDS AND PREFERENCES

Face it. There will be pain. How much? What type? How long you will feel it? That is all up to you. The more primitive part of your brain will likely lean towards options that are "perceived" to be less painful. I keep emphasizing the concept of perception. Here is the irony. There are few, if any, actual pain receptors in your brain. However, interpretation of pain occurs in the brain. If you stick your hand in a fire, the pain is not fully appreciated and understood until the messages traverse from your hand up through the spinal cord, through the lower brain and finally through your cerebral cortex.

Receiving a flu shot, a shot of Novocaine or an inoculation against a disease may be painful, but you tolerate it because you construct a mental rationale that it will protect you against future pain that could be far greater. *You are able to reduce the perception of pain (or at least tolerate it better) when you focus on thoughts that justify the short-term pain.*

This seems easier when an expert such as a doctor or a dentist tells you to do so. Why don't you trust the "expert" that is inside you? Why do you allow the exaggeration of future, unknown, imagined pain to sabotage your more rational thoughts about rising up from your hurt?

MONTE

Monte loved to shop for gadgets. He was an "early adopter" and wanted to be the first one of his friends to have each new advance in cell phones, televisions, computers and other "electronica." However, there was a small issue. Monte didn't earn enough money to pay for these purchases with cash. So he simply pulled out his credit card and charged these items. At month end, when the bills came in, Monte found himself paying huge interest payments on his debt.

Monte was not stupid, but when asked about why he continued to do this, he said that he just couldn't bear to see friends and colleagues have these new toys before he did. The idea that he couldn't have these toys was painful to him. Or was it? Was that the "real" issue? Maybe, it was easier for Monte to focus on electronic gadgetry than on the roots of his self-esteem.

Monte imagined that his friends would mock him and make fun of the fact that he didn't earn as much as they did. He thought that they would think less of him if he didn't have every new device, feature or application as soon as it came out. This perceived pain was too much for him to bear.

Paying exorbitant interest rates in the privacy of his own home, away from the glare of his friends, was more palatable than not having the newest devices. Monte had no long-term plan to escape from debt. The pain for Monte wasn't physical, but it was as debilitating as many other types of physical pain.

When deciding what type of pain you are willing to face, ask yourself some of these questions?

a) Which is more painful for you: physical suffering or mental suffering?
b) In the past, what types of pain were you willing to endure?
c) In the past, what types of pain were you not willing to endure?
d) What mental resources did you use to help you minimize your pain?
e) Are there any new resources that you would be willing to use this time around?

f) What thoughts, perceptions and support could you use to minimize the amount of pain you imagine?

Having a game plan to deal with anticipated pain will allow you to use amount of pain as a factor to select options in a more realistic way.

6) LEARNING NEW BEHAVIORS vs. ADAPTING OLD BEHAVIORS

When you look back at problems that you have faced and solved previously, you hopefully will realize that you have been successful more times than not. You have a strong lexicon of coping skills that you have used previously. You just don't think about them often.

The other situations may have been different. The new issue may have been different. BUT the coping skill was often the same. Personally, I am a very persistent person. Most New Yorkers are. It was a survival skill necessary just to get through the day. I now live in San Diego. At times, I find myself lapsing and losing focus when faced with current pressures of deadlines. I have to actively remind myself that I am the same person that has overcome many more difficult issues before.

Like most people I have a preference for using what I already have had success with when facing new issues. I have the confidence to believe that "old school rules" work well for me.

Perhaps you are different. Perhaps you have been less successful with your problem-solving techniques. Perhaps you don't have a lot of coping skills. Perhaps you are frustrated with using your old skills and are looking for a fresh, more objective, perspective on the problem. Perhaps you like to upgrade your skill set constantly with new and improved technology or methodology.

Recently, many people have found great solace in the "Laws of Attraction" and other wisdom contained in books like "The Secret." While I'm not sure that those concepts are really new, the new vocabulary and packaging have made those ideas exciting and accessible for many people currently looking for answers. Visualizing success may be helpful. However, unless it is coupled with action, it may not be sufficient to be successful.

One of my graduate school professors, a wizened European gentleman named Otto Weir once said, "There is nothing really new today. All of the ideas about how people behave have been stated many times in many different ways in many different cultures. People are just lazy and don't want to go back to the original classics to find the origins of these ideas." BUT it doesn't matter if it is new or not new anyway. All that matters is whether or not you are willing to commit to use these ideas when facing issues. There is no correct formula.

However, I do suggest that you spend some time thinking about what you did and didn't use in the past, just to make sure that you are considering the whole gamut of possibilities.

7) LEVEL OF SUPPORT AVAILABLE

Some people do better solving problems when they are surrounded by other people who are going through similar experiences. They feel less isolated and overwhelmed by the situation if they have other people who either have been there or are currently there. Programs such as Weight Watchers and Alcoholics Anonymous have long stressed the concept that receiving support from others in the same situation you are in is reassuring. It provides evidence and support that you can "do it" too.

However, some people choose to go it alone. They look disparagingly at other people with the same issues, particularly if their rate of change or desire and intensity for change is less than their own. They feel like the group is a heavy weight around their necks. Some people, for personal or cultural reasons, feel uncomfortable discussing their shortcomings in front of or with other people. In some cultures, the very concept of going to a therapist or a support group is a foreign concept.

In general, men are less likely than women to feel comfortable sharing their problems in the presence of others. Admitting to shortcomings is perceived as weak in their own eyes and is intolerable. Some men do not seek assistance from any type of support person or group until the issue has gotten extreme.

There are various different levels of support. From professional help to the advice and suggestions from family and friends. There are groups that meet one time only. There are groups that meet daily or weekly. In certain situations and occupations, peer discussions carry less stigma than seeking out the counsel of authority figures or corporate resources such as EAP's (Employee Assistance Programs).

Chatting can even be done online with peers, colleagues or professionals so that "no one can see your face." The safety of using a screen name instead of your actual name can reduce the discomfort of opening up about the issue.

There is no right answer. You should consider whether or not talking with others and listening to their insights can help you get a clearer perspective.

8) PUBLIC vs. PRIVATE ACTIVITY

Some people have a strong desire to tell others about the changes they want to make. They feel that by making a public commitment, they will strengthen their resolve to follow through. They feel that others will be able to help hold them accountable for what they have proposed. Some people write their goals down and post them in visible spaces to serve as a measuring stick to track their progress.

Other people are much more private about making changes. Some people will go to another city for cosmetic surgical procedures to keep others from finding out about what they are doing. In certain clinics, private waiting rooms have been established so that no one knows who else is seeking similar assistance from the doctor.

Many issues can affect the choice here. Cultural and religious background can be a strong influence. Family preferences can also impact these choices. Other issues include your level of self-esteem and locus of control. Self-esteem is concerned with how we feel about ourselves, while locus of control is concerned with whether or not we believe that we have great influence over the things that happen to us.

From a self-esteem perspective:
a) Who judges whether or not you are doing the right thing? You or others?
b) Who judges whether or not you are a good person? You or others?

From a locus of control perspective:
a) Who influences the things that happen to you? You or others?
b) Who has control over the things that happen to you? You or others?

These two concepts are often correlated with one another. In general, people with higher levels of self-esteem believe that they possess a higher degree of influence over what happens to them. They may be more likely to deal with their issues publicly, relatively unaffected by the judgment and influence of others. However, there are certainly exceptions and variations. In particular situations, people with high self-esteem may choose to be more private if they are concerned with being perceived as "posers" or "impostors."

When choosing to go public or stay private, there is no right and wrong answer.

9) DEPTH OF INQUIRY

Some people want only to solve the issue at hand, whereas others can view the emergence of the issue as an opportunity to inquire and introspect about much broader issues. Ultimately, the issues of "BEING" on the planet and "What's it all about?" are entwined with almost every problem.

Rising up from your hurt usually applies to the existing issue. However, solving that issue may open the doors to deeper inquiry. If the current issue has you feeling like you have hit "rock bottom," it may be easier to see the connectivity between the current issue and lifestyle issues and choices.

For years, clients had the ability in therapy to choose between in-depth analysis and short-term behavioral modification. Each served a clear purpose and found traction in the therapeutic community. Freudian psychoanalysis often involved daily or frequent weekly sessions with a therapist. The ground covered traced issues back to origins in childhood, believing that most modern problems were related to unresolved childhood feelings and stages. Jungian therapy focused on the integration of ego with other conscious and unconscious parts of the personality. This type of therapy could last for years. Although enlightening and intellectually stimulating, current issues were not necessarily addressed or addressed quickly.

Short-term behavioral therapies focused on remedying errant behavior without looking at underlying causes. The premise was that the behavior was the issue. What you see is what you get. These therapies eliminated issues more quickly because they did not inquire at any level below the conscious.

Rising up from your hurt suggests that you decide how far you want to go in solving the problem and understanding yourself. Going deeper takes more time, asks many more questions and perhaps costs more money (if you are seeking professional guidance.) However, the changes in resultant behavior may be more far reaching.

Do have the time, patience, persistence or interest?

10) LIKELIHOOD OF RELAPSE

Recidivism rates or the likelihood of relapse is an issue that is critical within our criminal justice system. Before and after a felon is released on parole, case workers are constantly trying to assess whether or not the person can make it. AlAnon and NarcAnon groups have their own predictors for the likelihood of continued drinking or drug use.

If we just change one issue in our lives, will that be enough to resist temptations, associations and friends from our past? Plenty of people have quit smoking, drinking and gambling cold turkey. Others have relapsed many times and have joined a never ending sequence of "Anon" groups.

What will you do? What does your own history suggest about your ability to resist temptation?

DAN

Dan started getting into trouble with progressively heavier and heavier drinking. After several DUI's, losing his job and his marriage, he could see that drinking was going to kill him, one way or another. Years in AlAnon and listening to others supported that belief.

However, while continuing to go to meetings, he turned to cocaine and started to use it weekly. He did not think of himself as an addict or user because in his words "he could take it or leave it." That was true in the beginning. He could leave it for a week, maybe two, particularly when he didn't have the cash to pay for it or when he had to find another dealer (when his previous dealer got arrested). However, soon he couldn't leave it for more than a few days, then not for a day and finally he needed it all the time. Several close calls and a near arrest brought him to NarcAnon, where he started in at Step One again.

If the story ended there, perhaps you wouldn't see a clear theme to Dan's life. On the way to NarcAnon meetings, Dan would stop at the local Indian Casino, at first, only to buy cheaper cigarettes. One day he threw a few coins into a slot machine. Much to his surprise, he won a jackpot that paid for 13 cartons of cigarettes.

Dan started to make more and more frequent trips to the casino, even when he didn't need cigarettes. He started to gamble most of his discretionary income and finally rent money and food money. All in search of another big jackpot. That's all he ever sought. THE NEXT BIG JACKPOT. When the money ran, out Dan was off to Gamblers Anonymous and there he was at Step One, yet one more time.

For Dan and perhaps many others like him, we should at least consider the concept of the "addictive personality." While there is considerable evidence as to the physiological and genetic roots to alcohol addiction and nicotine addiction, no one has yet found the gambling gene (although there is some physiological evidence about different levels of dopamine and serotonin in the brains of risk takers in general).

Some people have a "need" for something so compelling that it takes over their mind and body with ferocity. Whether it is shopping, eating, sexual activity or sports mania, that interest begins to drive their life. It becomes their "raison d'etre." Life is always focused on getting "the next fix" or "the next jackpot." For these people, life becomes a sequence of choices where their locus of control is not very high. In other words, they are not in control of their choices. Instead, their choices control every aspect of their lives.

There are choices made that are less destructive and possibly even nurturing. Some people find religion, painting, poetry and community service to be their "drug of choice." While these are certainly more socially acceptable with far fewer socially and economically destructive consequences, they can take over a person's life just as easily. Sit down with new, fervent and committed believers to see how long they can go without invoking their "calling."

If you have an addictive personality, you may simply resign yourself to a series of addictions, hopefully making choices with progressively less destructiveness attached to each and every one.

You may choose to CAREFRONT yourself, check your locus of control and seek to understand the role that these addictions play in your life. For many people, the addiction is what makes life worth living. It is so hooked into their SELF CONCEPT that life without the "current" addiction seems pointless and barren.

OR

YOU CAN LEARN TO LIVE A DIFFERENT LIFE, where you have more control over the choices that you make. *THE KEY ELEMENT IS THAT THE CHOICE IS IN YOUR HANDS.*

***

Using the list above, choose those factors (and feel free to come up with others) that you will use to evaluate the options that you will learn to find in the next chapter. Feel free to use any of the 10 factors I have suggested here or choose other factors that fit your SELF CONCEPT and issue. Just pick factors based on their ability to help you change. As long as they are working for you, stick to them.

Chapter 13

OPTION THINKING

Linear thinking and Option Thinking are two different approaches to problem solving. Our school system does a reasonably good job at teaching people to think in a linear, logical fashion. The main goal of this kind of thinking is to find the "right" answer. The faster, the better. The less peripheral sidetracking, the better. No reason to waste time on anything other than honing in on the "right" answer quickly. Other speculation is viewed as extraneous and unnecessary.

The process that characterizes linear thinking is like a funnel. You pour data into the wide opening, crunch it down and then the optimal answer, the proverbial "bottom line," appears out of the narrow end. In a more predictable, less changing and volatile personal or organizational world, the efficiencies of this type of process might counterbalance the potential disadvantages.

What are the disadvantages of linear thinking?

There are at least 5 potential issues:

1) In linear thinking, once you find the "right" answer, you stop looking for or even considering that there could be other equally reasonable answers. You resent those who do not accept your "right" answer. You argue in favor of what you believe to be correct, while wearing blinders to most other possibilities.

2) During less volatile times, this "right answer" may actually be "right" for a period of time. If your world is fairly stable and constant and you have no real issues, the life expectancy of your "right" answer is longer. In this century, however, we have seen non-stop, whirlwind change. Business models have had to change. Things that were "so right" for "so long" are now "so wrong".

When you are wrestling with an issue, holding onto the previous "right" answers, without periodically reconsidering them, can cause a lot of personal pain.

3) Linear thinking assumes that you, the world we live in and your issue is a logical issue. While it may have a logical element to it, rising up from your hurt emphasizes looking at issues from an emotional perspective first and then proceeding with a more logic-based view of the issue. Think about it this way. When we try to apply logic to emotional issues, it tends to infuriate the person who is in the midst of emotional turmoil.

Let me offer an example. In many relationships, one person is more emotional, while the other is more logical. There is nothing inherently wrong or problematic with this, until the emotional person has an issue.

In male-female relationships, women (for a variety of reasons) tend to be more emotional than their male counterparts. I personally believe this to be a good thing. When I try to explain this to women, I tell them it may be helpful to view men as well-intentioned but operating from a more logic-based perspective.

If the woman comes home upset about something that has happened during the day and relates this to her male partner, he will respond by doing what he "thinks" will make her feel better. Therefore, he will first logically explain to her why she shouldn't be upset in the first place. Often, he unwittingly implies that she has caused her own upset by not being logical.

Most women will listen to this and think, "How did I get involved with this man in the first place?" He views it as a logical issue, while she feels that it is an emotional issue. Consequently, he doesn't provide the active listening and empathy that she is seeking.

Seeing that this first reaction has not solved the situation, the man will then offer to "help to fix the problem," despite the fact that this is NOT what the woman asked for. He is subtly implying that, since she can't solve the problem by herself, he will do it for her. In return, he expects to be rewarded and appreciated, while the woman feels completely misunderstood. The best way to deal with this situation is to simply have a conversation about the different ways in which you both look at the situation. Easier said than done. Still, being able to address a problem at its emotional core first will allow all parties to move forward towards addressing the problem from a more logical perspective more effectively.

4) Linear thinking tends to value what you know to be true from the past. It is more "evidence based" than Option Thinking, insofar as Option Thinking tends to be optimistic, forward looking and more open to considering new behaviors. Using linear thinking is the equivalent of getting into your car and driving, by mainly paying attention to what is in your rear view mirror. It is great to know where you have been and what is coming up quickly from behind, but it is not so terrific when it comes to driving full speed ahead. Option thinking tends to be more proactive and focused on more possibilities for the future.

5) Even if you end up with the same answer, it is better to have used Option Thinking because you have usually considered a wider set of possibilities in reaching your conclusion. Additionally, when the world changes (and it will), you won't have to re-evaluate the data and search for the new "right" answer since you'll already have it in your list of options. You can choose from Option B, C, D, E or?, because you were prepared for the inevitable changes.

Now that you have a clearer idea about what linear thinking may look like, let's take a look at Option Thinking. I mentioned earlier that our traditional educational system has depended primarily upon linear thinking. However, the most recent Common Core curriculum, in place in our children's schools today, is an attempt to help refocus thinking more along the lines of Option Thinking. The idea is no longer about getting exactly the right answer but more about thinking through the ways to get there.

At its core, Option Thinking is significantly different from linear thinking in four ways:

1) The number of options that you look for in option thinking is greater than the number you look for in linear thinking.

2) The order in which you identify the options in option thinking is different and in the beginning seems counterintuitive.

3) A spirit of optimism and endless possibility pervades Option Thinking.

4) Option Thinking places considerable emphasis on how you view your old assumptions, ask questions, and "reframe the problem."

Option Thinking will teach you 10 ideas that can change the way you think FOREVER:

1) Never settle for 1 or 2 options. Don't make critical decisions unless you have identified at least 3-5 options.

2) Don't start your thinking with Worst Case Scenarios. There is plenty of time for that after you have considered Best Case Scenarios. Since you aren't likely to use either of these scenarios since each is so extreme, make sure you also search for Most Probable Case Scenarios. If you have PLANS "D, E and F" (Options 4,5 and 6) in your back pocket, you will feel more in control, have less stress and be able to choose from a wider array of Options.

3) Whenever you feel STUCK, know that there are many methods to get UNSTUCK (see Chapter 11). When you are STUCK, you rarely make the best decisions. Having options available to you will to get UNSTUCK as soon as you recognize the need to employ different strategies.

4) Most people don't challenge their assumptions about the issue and possible Options. Unwarranted and untested assumptions typically lead to foregone conclusions. You assume that the world will continue to behave as it has always behaved, which in today's world is a very bad and dangerous notion. The world is in the midst of constant, paradigm shifting change. The one thing you know for sure is that yesterday's answers should be thoroughly reviewed to determine if they are relevant and still work.

5) Most people don't ask enough questions about the issue. They don't test the limits, scope or parameters of the issue. The best problem solvers are the people who can ask the most and the best questions. Asking the "unaskable" questions can lead to the "unsayable" answer. Don't be in a rush when it comes to asking questions. Asking more questions can help to uncover options that were previously hidden or overlooked along the way, thus increasing the chances that you come upon more workable and effective options.

6) Most problems are poorly stated. Sometimes, what you think is the issue isn't the real issue. It is a symptom of another issue that you may not have even thought about yet. Don't be so quick to solve the issue as stated. There may be a better way to state the issue that could lead to lots of different, more palatable options.

7) Sometimes none of the options that you have seem palatable. They each carry with them another set of issues that await solution. There are times when your only real choice is which of the "next set" of issues/problems, you prefer to deal with.

8) Make sure that the first Option you consider is unusual. Hunter Thompson said it best when he stated, "When the going gets weird, the weird turn professional." The purpose of the first Option is NOT to solve the problem. It is to increase the bandwidth of the problem and to stimulate new, courageous and different thinking.

9) Remember that Best Case Scenarios and Worst Case Scenarios can flip flop and change dramatically when we use different criteria to evaluate them. Always establish the way you will choose to evaluate Options BEFORE you think of Options. (Refer back to Chapter 12: How to Decide Which Option is Best for You.)

10) It is critical to understand that emotions as well as logic will influence your criteria, assumptions, questions, options and issue statements. It would be nice if we all made decisions in a logical way.

However, since you make decisions based on emotions, address the emotional aspect of the matter first and then justify those decisions with logic. This idea alone is worth the price of this book.

Here are 4 tent poles or cornerstones to help you grasp what Option Thinking can do for you.

1) The starting point for Option Thinking is always Best Case Scenario (BCS), not Worst Case Scenario (WCS). During tough times and in the midst of tough situations, the default mode of thinking is to consider WCS first. Why?

    a) It happens. It may even happen most of the time, but that is still not a good reason to consider it first. If you start with WCS, you rarely ever return to BCS. This sucks all of the optimism out of your thought process. There is no blue sky, only clouds. Also when asked for a back-up option, you start to conjure up WTTCS (Worse Than That Case Scenario), just to show that WCS wasn't so horrible in the first place.

    b) It allows for CYA (Cover Your "Hindquarters") behavior. Cautious people think that once the hindquarters are covered, they are protected and insulated from bad things. To an extent this is true, but the analogy is that when an ostrich sticks his/her head in the ground, it is still exposed. She/he may not realize it, but anyone watching can easily see it.

    c) If you end up choosing a slightly better option than WCS, you can feel smug about the fact that it could have been "worse." It is a way to elevate an unpalatable option. If you have a terrible job and your boss tells you that you are lucky to have a job at all, compared to the legions of unemployed, will you be any more thrilled about this bad job? If your doctor tells you that you are sick and you complain, he may say, "Well at least you're not dying." Will that make being sick more acceptable to you?

So then why should we consider BCS first, particularly when it is highly unlikely to occur?

When you are free to think on your own, your thoughts often begin with "Wouldn't it be nice IF..." Whether this is done in order to feel good or because it is a beautiful escape from current pressures is not important. What is important is that the initial idea can set the emotional tempo for future thinking.

In good times, you want to investigate all possibilities because you can afford to. You are not under pressure to "DO" something. The irony is that during tough times or when an issue arises, it is even more important for you to do so. You should be thinking in exactly the same way, but somehow you feel that you can't afford to.

Instead of looking at the world with an "abundance" mentality, you develop a "scarcity/hoarder" mentality. This dramatically colors the options you may consider. Why should your thought process change as a function of whether or not you are facing an issue? Maybe the final decision you make will be different in a problematic situation, but the thought process should be consistent. Don't allow your thought process to change just because of the issue at hand.

It is a goal or a target. It provides you with something to shoot for. Hopefully, it opens up the possibilities for you to consider more options. In the long run, when you see more options and have a larger solution set to choose from, you will make better decisions. Also, if the first option is truly unusual, it can spark more original thinking.

If you have been to college, you have probably heard the following study. Two teachers were given the same class of children. One teacher was told that the children were very bright. The other teacher was told that the children were "human speed bumps." (It took them an hour and a half to watch 60 minutes.) There should be no surprise as to which group of children did better. If the teacher thought that the children were bright, she/he treated them differently, and naturally the children performed better, even though they were no different than the other group of children.

If you were going to sell your home, you wouldn't start off by telling the potential buyer the lowest price you would accept, would you? If you expect more, you tend to get more. I am not advocating putting unreasonable expectations on yourself. However, goals which include a strong, optimistic vision of tomorrow that are within reach are probably better than goals strictly focused on today.

The strongest reason to start with BCS is that, even if we can't utilize a full-blown BCS, we may be able to use selected parts of it. When an organization looks at "Best in Class" practices, it is trying to copy what practices the best follow and integrate that thinking into what the organization's currently doing, even if it is not operating at a very high level right now.

Imagine if you could just use one piece of a BCS in whatever you are doing to help you rise up from your hurt. Wouldn't that be an upgrade? Finding small parts of a BCS that you can use, even if you settle for using a WCS, could become one of your goals.

Think of a BCS as the door opener to all the possibilities. It can color your entire realm of thought with optimism. Starting your thinking off with what you find to be reasonable and feasible may seem prudent from a linear point of view, but it conjures up an emotional feeling of grim resignation as opposed to unbridled hope. It is this spirit of hope that provides us with the emotional fuel to want to "chart new territory." "Out with the old and in with more of the old" is a poor alternative to fresh thinking.

2) The second critical tent pole involves expanding the quantity and quality of Options. The first option considered should open up unexplored vistas by wandering into uncharted territory. Even if you can't do the first "far out" option, it allows you to see the Blue Sky and begin to wonder "what if." Human Factors research tells us that people can typically consider 3-7 options simultaneously (younger people can probably consider 9 or 10) and maintain several perspectives on an issue at the same time. Option Thinking allows you to look at the problem under a microscope and then rise to the10, 000-foot level to get a different view just by changing vantage points used to evaluate options or by using different perspectives.

Having more options also gives you the illusion of control (if not actual control) and reduces the stress of being stuck between the rock and the hard place. When I teach stress prevention and change management, I always mention that the difference between the people who thrive on stress and change and those who are crippled by stress and change is simple. It usually is a function of who can see endless opportunities versus who can see endless problems. You probably like change when you have an increased number of options. You probably don't like change when you feel that there aren't many good options.

Option Thinking also provides back-up plans in terms of other options that are considered during the initial thought process but don't get immediately selected for action. Having Plan "B" is nice to have when Plan "A" has to be scrapped. Wouldn't it be nicer to have Plans "C," "D" and "E" in your back pocket ready to go as well? When your world changes again, and it will, who will be able to react better? The person with the "right answer" or the person who has 5-7 options?

3) The third tent pole involves what we do with untested assumptions and how we use questions. Linear people are more comfortable relying on time tested assumptions that they have always used. Some of these assumptions are based on "old scripts," that were once useful but have not been updated. The problem is that you don't regularly review all of the assumptions that guide the way you behave. You are not even aware of many of them, which presents an even bigger problem.

DAVE

Dave has always been shy around women. In the back of his mind, lost over time, is an incident that still drives Dave's current behavior. When he was10 years old, he wanted to talk to a girl in his class, Darla. Darla was probably equally uncomfortable but more verbal and assertive. When Dave said something that he found funny to Darla, she called him a "stupidhead." Dave never forgot that. Dave created a script for himself that talking to girls was dangerous (at least to his ego.)

Over the years, Dave forgot about this triggering event but still maintains the behavior. Now that he is single again, he is uncomfortable about starting to date. Checking out his assumptions and the payoffs for being shy (such as not risking being embarrassed again) could go a long way in helping Dave to move forward.

PAT

Ellen is unhappy that her boyfriend Pat chews food with his mouth open. Pat, being a typical male, has no idea that he is even doing this. Ellen is reluctant to tell Pat about this because "she doesn't want to hurt Pat's feelings." Or so she says. Instead, she engages in passive aggressive behavior by looking away or rolling her eyes whenever he does this.

In the long run, she hurts Pat's feelings more by not explaining her withdrawal behavior. Pat doesn't understand it and just assumes that Ellen is "in one of her moods." Pat has never tested her assumption that, if she says something critical to Pat about his behavior, he may turn around and offer a criticism of something that she is doing.

In Option Thinking, it is important to list your assumptions that may impact your issue. Challenge them. Reality test them. A behavior on the surface may seem perfectly logical. However, it may really be a façade or masquerade for something hidden. It could be a defense mechanism. It could be the tip of an iceberg. It could be a symptom of another issue. There is no way to know for sure, until you ask yourself lots of questions:

a) How long have I been doing this?

b) Is it working well for me?

c) Do I remember why I started doing this?

d) Who else could help me to remember when and why I started doing this?

e) What other behaviors did I even try, in addition to this behavior?

f) What other possibilities are there?

There are probably a whole host of other "What If" questions you could ask as well.

Option Thinking encourages you to state and test your assumptions about the issue and possible solutions regularly. Rather than just accept and collude to ignore the "elephants in the room," Option Thinking encourages you to "ask the unaskable." Option Thinking encourages you to "say the unsayable." Option Thinking encourages you to tell The TRUTH. Option Thinking demands that you constantly ask questions and pose "what ifs." Sometimes the best questions are the ones that are so basic that, in the midst of the issue, you would rarely even think to ask those questions.

4) The last tent pole focuses on the definition of the issue itself. OT seeks to find optimal statements of issues as opposed to attempting to solve issues exactly in the way they are presented by the world. When issues arise, you may just become uncomfortable about even having the issue.

You do not see the issue as an opportunity for growth. Instead, you view it negatively and seek to eliminate it, reduce it or ignore it. You rarely question the issue to see if it is the "real" issue or just a symptom of a bigger issue. You don't question the issue or challenge the issue. It is just accepted as stated, even though there might be an alternative or easier way to deal with it.

Growth typically occurs when you are not comfortable AND have an issue. When you are happy, there is no "hunger" or sense of urgency about growth. When you are in pain, you may start the process of "deeper inquiry" or face a new challenge. This can result in rapid personal growth.

Let's apply this same concept of "reframing" to 2 real world issues. For the past several years, you have heard great concerns about:

1) reducing violence in the workplace (e.g. the Post Office)

and

2) reducing violence in our schools and college campuses.

Each of these issues is complex and has no easy answers. However, they are also poorly problems stated: "too late into the process." By the time a postal worker or high school student picks up a weapon and has decided to shoot someone, there is very little anyone could do.

Here are but a few of the ideas that I have heard to help deal with this problem:

1) Put metal detectors in schools and Post Office buildings to prevent weapons from being brought inside. This may just shift the homicidal person to choose another type of non-metallic weapon (e.g. a plastic pipe bomb, material to start a fire and/or explosion.)

2) Train principals/guidance counselors or in-lobby postal supervisors in crisis management techniques equivalent to the strategies taught

to hostage negotiators. Not to denigrate the skills and talent level of those fine men and women, but once a person has generated that degree of anger, even highly skilled professionals would have a hard time defusing the situation. You could use fully licensed psychologists, psychiatrists, social workers or any other mental health professional, and their odds would not be much better in reducing the violence at the flashpoint.

3) Install security cameras everywhere and monitor them constantly to detect suspicious behavior. From a cost and invasion of privacy perspective, this solution seems like overkill.

All of these options are costly, with low probabilities of success in attending to the violence problem. The main reason they would not work well is that they are trying to stop the behavior as the worst possible time, right when the perpetrator is at his/her peak of anger, frustration or hurt.

The original problem statement was:

How can violence in the workplace or the school be reduced?

If we "reframe" the problem, we can instead ask:

How can we identify students/employees when they are starting to or continuing to become withdrawn, detached, sad, angry, hurt or frustrated, BEFORE they feel the need to become violent?

That would open up many lower cost, higher probability of success, options:

1) Inoculate students/employees with education, information and suggestions about coping skills before they need them;

2) Train peers to recognize "disconnecting" behavior and learning how to offer care and concern;

3) Create buddy systems where each student/employee has at least one other person to talk to, lean on and confide in;

4) Create environments within schools/workplaces where employees can go to vent frustrations (e.g., rooms where employees can go to yell and scream, beat on punching bags or rip up trash)

5) Create environments where feelings such as hurt, anger and frustration can be vented to concerned, non-judgmental others.

These options do not guarantee that there will be no violence in the schools/workplace. They do, however, open up the conversation about attacking the issue when it is still in the formative stage, rather than when it has reached the flash point. Issues dealt with when they are smaller "itches" are more amenable to intervention than when they are full blown.

Some of these suggestions have already been implemented in schools to reduce violence, notably the training and use of peer intervention. It has been reported that fellow students at Columbine High School in Colorado knew that their violent classmates were "disconnected" and "planning something." They just weren't sure what to do when they first heard about it. Too bad these programs were not in existence at the time of need.

Now that you have learned about Option Thinking, let's use it to better understand some of the cases that were discussed earlier.

Let's go back to Chapter 6 to revisit Cathy and Bruce. What is Cathy's problem? Is it that she doesn't have enough time to meet all of the expectations that she has placed on herself in her life? Is it her concept of what being a "good mother" and a "good teacher" are? Maybe it is her current set of priorities? How about her idea of what being "selfish" and "selfless" is? There are other old scripts that she can reconsider as well (just reread the chapter, if you don't remember her situation.)

Remember Bruce. What is Bruce's problem? Is it a lack of excitement and FUN in his life? Is it a lack of intimacy? Is it that Bruce does not have many friends in his new environment? Maybe it is that Bruce hasn't grown as fast or in the same direction as Emily? Perhaps it is just a lack of communication issue. It is also possible that having married so young that they are experiencing the "7-year itch" or have just fallen out of love.

All of these are ways of looking at the issues that are causing both of them concern and dismay. Solving any of these issues will bring Cathy and Bruce a modicum of relief.

What is the BEST way of looking at her/his problem? What do you think?

If either of them just changes one element of his/her behavior, without understanding the "payoffs," what guarantee does either one of them have that another symptomatic behavior won't arise? None.

Let me offer a "reframe" for Cathy and Bruce to consider. Perhaps this is as good a time as any for Cathy/Bruce to sit down and ask herself/

himself: "Who am I?" For Cathy and Bruce and many people like them, people live day by day without ever really reconsidering old scripts and choices that they made many years ago. Who are they at this exact moment in life? What really matters to each of them?

Some of us are so busy living life on a day-to-day basis that we rarely take the time to consider these issues. We just see ourselves in terms of the roles that we play. Cathy has evolved into her current roles as wife, mother, teacher, friend and pet owner, but who is Cathy at her core? What is her "SELF CONCEPT?" What is really important to her? What is she doing on the planet?

Bruce has evolved into his roles as husband, provider, employee and friend, but who is Bruce at his core? What is his "SELF CONCEPT?" What is really important to him? What is he doing on the planet?

Thinking about these more weighty issues may not bring immediate relief to Cathy/Bruce and their surface issues. However, opening up that avenue of inquiry will allow each of them to bring a new perspective to the issue regardless of which problem he/she chooses to deal with. Those of us with clearer ideas about "who we are," can usually separate out problems and options in a better manner.

Cathy and Bruce will reach one set of conclusions if she/he continues to define herself/himself only according to the roles that they play for others. He/she may reach a completely different set of conclusions, if she/he defines herself/himself first, in terms of who he/she is on the planet.

Think of YOUR issue and how YOU have defined it. Have you defined it in terms of your day to day life or within a larger context? Do YOU know who YOU are? What are YOU doing on the planet? Perhaps reconsidering this issue for yourself will help you to "reframe" YOUR issue.

Option Thinking has the potential to change the way you see YOURSELF, your environment, your choices and the way YOU live your life. Many of YOU who have chosen to read this book only as a tool to rise up from your hurt can now recognize the greater potential of deeper inquiry.

Chapter 14

THE ART OF ASKING QUESTIONS

What do the BEST Leaders and the BEST Salespeople have in common? They ask the BEST questions. This is equally true of people who are good at rising up from their hurt. Asking questions gives you the best opportunities to:

1) Challenge assumptions
2) Uncover unseen problem elements
3) Reality test your beliefs
4) See a problem at multiple levels
5) "Reframe" the problem and/or possible solutions.

Questions also serve five other purposes:

1) Demonstrating to yourself that you are open to the process of inquiry about your issue. Acknowledging that there is an issue, which may be more complicated than you thought, is a big first step. You may not be as afraid of asking the question as you are about possibly finding the answer. "Don't ask, Don't Tell" works as well for you when you have an issue as it does in the US Army. Once you start asking the questions, the real issues may surface.

2) Setting an optimistic tone to the inquiry is equally important. If you view the process as a growth opportunity, then you can rise up from your hurt faster. PMA (Positive Mental Attitude) can speed up the process.

3) Asking questions can help you to build momentum to overcome your current state of inertia. Asking questions can become YOUR UNBALANCED FORCE that gets you started. The process of

opening your inquiry may show you that the journey is not nearly as scary or daunting as you may have originally thought.

4) Asking "What If" questions allows you to imagine possible scenarios without fully committing to them. It allows you to float "trial balloons" into the atmosphere of your imagination to see what happens. What would your life be like if you no longer had this issue? How much more energy could you have to pursue other interests? Speculating about these issues could serve as the initial UNBALANCED FORCE for you. It could also serve to refortify yourself.

5) Asking questions also allows you to consider outrageous possibilities without really taking complete ownership of them. During Medieval times, the court jester would pop into discussions and question/mock the lord of the manor in a way that few others would dare. Because he/she was considered the fool, no one took the question or taunt all that seriously. However, the unusual thought was at least introduced into the conversation. Even if the thought was only considered at a subliminal level, it was at least considered.

A "silly" question potentially becomes a "seed" which may or not may not flourish when watered and fertilized with other ideas in the future. You need a court jester in your own brain who periodically jumps into your consciousness and screams at you, "What are you doing? Why are you doing that?"

Considering what might at first glance seem outrageous is a great way of expanding your option set. It is considerably more difficult to rise up from your hurt if you aren't willing to ask questions. Lots of them. The more, the better. The more unusual, the better. If you can't think of questions to ask yourself, maybe other people can ask you questions.

Asking a question humbles you by showing you that maybe you don't have all the answers at this moment AND THAT IT IS OK not to have all of the answers at this moment. It opens up your curiosity to see what has been familiar to you for so long as novel, unusual or even strange. That gets your creative juices flowing and contributes to your ability to rise up from your hurt.

Questions are a palatable way in which to "Think the UnThinkable" and "Say the UnSayable." They can allow you to gain access to previously secret and unreachable areas of your mind. The concept is that if you can "Ask the UnAskable," perhaps you can "Do the UnDoable." That is the primary reason why questions provide the catalyst to speed up problem resolution and rise up from your hurt.

Chapter 15

OVERCOMING FEAR OF FAILURE: SSPS (SUCCESSFUL SEQUENTIAL PROBLEM SOLVING)

The critical factor that keeps you from attempting new behaviors is FEAR. It is actually a special type of FEAR that I call FOF (Fear of Failure). Even though what you are currently doing isn't working very well, at least you know how to do that. You have the illusion of competence. You have been doing this for a long time, so there must be something good/positive about it.

To maintain this illusion, you tell yourself that your situation isn't so bad. Others have it far worse. There aren't any simple answers to what ails you. This belief also supports you when you "catastrophize" the situation as extremely difficult, if not impossible, to change.

To attempt a new behavior, you will have to risk FAILURE, not that failure is such a bad thing. In fact, failure is what helps to change the hard wiring of your brain. Only through failure can people make successive approximations towards a pathway of success. Failure is merely the first step on the road to success.

That may be hard to hear when you are hurting. You reject that idea and perceive failure of a new behavior as worse than never having tried the new behavior in the first place. How sad. And paralyzing.

What is the antidote for Failure? Why Success, of course. Before you start talking about chickens and eggs, let me clarify. Failure and success are perceptions of reality. They are variations as to how we perceive our world. While there are real world rewards and consequences for both of them, it is really important to check out how you look at these two ideas.

For some people, success is measured by winning as opposed to losing, by doing better than the others around you. There are many adages supporting this.

1) Winning isn't everything. It is the only thing.
2) He who dies with the most toys wins.
3) There are winners, and then there is everyone else.
4) The only people who don't care about winning are losers.
5) Winning is all that matters.

But is that really what success is? For some of us, success can be measured more by the journey than by the final destination. Success can be having "fought the good fight." It can be described as having "left everything out there on the field of combat." It can be perceived as exceeding what we thought we were capable of. It can be seen as a step or two in the right direction. It can be viewed as delight just for having participated in the process.

These definitions are usually only acceptable to someone who has already achieved some success in the world. Or to someone who has matured and no longer needs to see everything as a competition. Or to someone who has not succeeded much at all and is just getting started. These definitions are typically not palatable to someone who is hurting or who is in the midst of an issue. Those filters can color the definition of success dramatically.

To you, Success and Failure may be two giant choices with little in between. You live with a digital perception in a largely analog world. You are so worried about the specter of failure that you rarely want to risk trying a new behavior unless the probability for reaching success is very high and perceived as "not that tough."

Therein, lies the answer. People with problems have tried many strategies to overcome FOF. Which of the following have you tried?

1) Positive mental attitude affirmations
2) Mental visualization of successful behaviors
3) Relaxation techniques to reduce the anxiety of trying new behaviors
4) support groups consisting of others who are experiencing the same turmoil that you are

5) Other self-help books
6) Cheerleading from people close to you
7) Law of attraction activities?

How are they working for you? If they were working for you, perhaps you would not be reading this book right now. You feel that if you could just take that first, second and/or third step and be successful, then maybe this time it would be different. I agree.

The ultimate antidote for Failure is Success. Is it possible to structure Success into the journey? Yes it is, as long as you are willing to try to achieve "inch "stones instead of milestones.

MICAH

Early in my career, when I was 24 years old, I had the privilege of becoming a principal of an elementary school. You may ask, "How did you become a principal at such an early age?" It was a private school, instead of a public school.

In the private school system, the requirements to become a principal are quite different. Since money was tight, the Board of Directors at the school looked for someone whom they perceived as bright, who had been an elementary school teacher and who could handle middle class and upper class parents who were paying good money to have their children educated. They wanted someone to do all of these things for very little compensation. I was 24, didn't know any better, and took the job.

At the school, we had a little 8-year-old boy, Micah, who was clearly not the sharpest pencil in the box. He wasn't stupid, but he wasn't Albert Einstein either. He was in the 3rd grade. What he didn't like in 3rd grade was Social Studies. In case you don't remember 3rd grade Social Studies, let me give you a quick review: Columbus, Nina, Pinta, Santa Maria, Washington, Franklin, Revolutionary War, Lincoln, and Civil War That's it. End of 3rd grade Social Studies. Certainly not rocket science.

What Micah really didn't like was taking tests in Social Studies. Each time a test came around, Micah would look at the first question. If he couldn't answer that, he would look at the last question. If he couldn't answer that, he would tear his paper. He was actually quite logical.

Micah knew that his parents, Mr. and Mrs. Primitivo, would beat the living daylights out of him if he failed a test. (This was back in the time when it was acceptable to hit your children as punishment.) Therefore, if he thought that he might fail, he simply opted not to take the test. You and I might have reached a similar conclusion if we had had to endure his parents.

This was a near classic example of FOF, in this case manifesting itself as test anxiety. We called his parents in to talk about what to do. Their response was predictable. They said, "No problem. Just beat him in school when he fails the next test and that will teach him." I replied by telling them, "We don't believe in that, and we don't do that at this school. It is not consistent with how we think kids learn."

How did we get Micah to take tests in Social Studies? Whenever I ask this question at a presentation, I always get the same set of answers:

1) Don't tell him it is a test.

(You know there are tests in the world. I want there to be tests of competence. Micah will have to take tests for the rest of his academic career and maybe beyond, so we will have to tell him that this IS A TEST.)

2) Let him take the test orally.

(I love that one. Now we can add public humiliation to what is already a desperate situation for him.)

3) Tell him that he is smart enough to do well on the test to build up his confidence.

(Telling him that he is going to do well doesn't easily erase the picture of Mom and/or Dad hitting him with a strap.)

None of these suggestions would do much good. Remember that the only antidote for FAILURE is SUCCESS, so we had to figure out how we were going to increase his chances of success.

How about by starting with a very easy question, such as "What nationality was Jimmy the Greek?" After Micah gets that one right, he will go to the last question. How about using: "What color was George Washington's white horse?" Bingo. Two for Two.

One more relatively easy question at the beginning of the test and his thoughts of failure and beatings will have diminished. Now his natural ability will take over, instead of his fear response. He knows that he is on the road to success.

Psychologists know that once a person has had a string of three running successes, his/her thoughts about failure are reduced. By structuring success into the journey, we may help him overcome his concerns about failure.

REBECCA

Like any good parent, I wanted my daughter Rebecca to learn to swim at a young age. I had her in the pool before she was a year old, and she was happy and unafraid as she swam.

By the time, she was four, I told her that I would now teach her to swim under water. She would have to put her entire head under the water, hold her breath and then swim. A look of fear flashed on her face.

There is a lesson in this. Whenever you ask someone or even YOURSELF to do something and the automatic knee jerk answer of "no/ no way" is the response, it should tell you that the person saying this is afraid of something. Fear has raised its ugly head again.

When I asked Rebecca what was making her afraid, she responded with "Nothing." Another sure sign that fear was present. What would a four year old be afraid of? Don't say drowning. That is an adult idea. Few four year olds know what drowning is. Perhaps she was afraid of monsters or sharks. We were swimming in a pool, so that wasn't likely. How about that she would sink to the bottom of the pool? Maybe she was concerned about not being able to see and bumping her head against the side of the pool? All of these are at least within the realm of possibilities.

Have you ever watched Saturday morning cartoons with your children? Have you ever seen what happens to a cartoon character, other than Sponge Bob and his friends, when they go into the water? Water fills up inside of their head, and, when they come out, the water flies out through a variety of orifices in the head. To an adult, this is just silly. To a small child, this may be scary. They don't know how to get the water out of their head. No one has taught them how to do that.

After much questioning, Rebecca finally blurted out in an exasperated way, "Look, I have seven holes in my head. Water is going to fill up my head, and that will be the end of me." In case you haven't counted the holes in your head recently, you have 2 eyes, 2 ears, 2 nostrils and a mouth. The good news is that at least she could count to seven. The bad news was that there was no way/no how that she was going to put her head under the water.

Most dads would have responded in the typical Dad way. They would have hurled poor Rebecca into the pool. After all, that is probably how they learned to swim. And Rebecca may have quickly learned that she could swim under water and that her head did not fill up with water. Then again, she might have hated Dad (an unacceptable option for me) and never gone into the pool again. I wasn't willing to take that chance.

The logical readers would probably have taken out a medical textbook and pointed out features such as ear drums, nasal membranes and eyelids, all designed to keep water out of the head. Typical of logical people -- trying to solve an EMOTIONAL issue with LOGIC. Remember I said earlier that using logic to deal with an emotional issue only serves to annoy emotional people.

What would YOU have done if you had wanted her to have a success experience the very first time she put her head under the water. Remember, you are looking for inch stones or centimeter stones, not mile stones.

Here's what I did. I went to the local pharmacy and bought EACH OF US a pair of eye goggles, nose clips and a set of ear plugs. I put them on myself and took Rebecca over to the full length mirror in her room. I showed her how to put her set on and then asked her to look at herself in the mirror. I asked her to check the holes in her head and see if they were covered. She said, "Well it looks like 6 holes are covered. What about my mouth?" I said, "Keep that shut, and we'll be fine. We both looked a bit like goons, but the holes in her head were no longer an issue. I asked her if she was ready to swim underwater, and she tentatively said she would give it a go.

She looked a bit goofy but swam like a fish the first time out. Why? She was no longer thinking about FAILURE. She could see clearly with the goggles and loved the idea of fishing things up from the bottom of the pool. Shortly after, she pulled out the ear plugs, because she didn't like them. The nose clip followed after that. She kept the goggles on so that she could see clearer.

The conclusion to the story is that if I ask her today, "Rebecca, do you remember when you were afraid to put your head under the water?" Her response would be, "Dad, I was never afraid." She NEVER HAD TO EXPERIENCE THE FEAR because it was taken out of the situation before she could experience it.

Wouldn't it be terrific if someone were around to do that for you each and every time you were afraid? Someone is around, and that person is YOU. If you structure your approach to new behaviors in a way where you can guarantee success in the initial steps, your thoughts about FAILURE might diminish as well.

Let's go back and apply SSPS to the stories of Nancy and Teddy in Chapter 10. Nancy was famous for her yoyo diets, while Teddy bit his nails whenever he was late. Nancy could realize that her inability to lose weight had more to do with how she felt about herself than about the food she was eating.

The pivotal issue for her tended to arise when she was sitting around her living room at night not feeling terrific about herself. She would wander into the kitchen and begin to "eat" her troubled thoughts away.

Since we want Nancy to have success right away to help her overcome the looming feeling of FOF, it would be important for her to develop a list of activities that she could turn to in the evenings when she wasn't feeling good about herself.

That list might include activities such as:

1) Using a three-sentence mantra that she could say to comfort herself. "Right now, I am not happy with myself. This feeling will pass quickly because I am going to do something right now that will make me feel better. Tomorrow is a new day filled with opportunities for me to improve my life."

2) Having a "buddy/relative/friend/designated support person" whom she can call. This buddy will tell her how much she is cared for and appreciated.

3) Drawing a warm bath, lighting scented candles, putting on soft music and luxuriating in the feel, smell and sounds of her experience.

4) Going outside to sit on her patio and watch the stars in the moonlit sky.

5) Writing her thoughts in a journal and rereading them the next day to put them in perspective.

6) Turning on a favorite piece of music, adjusting her headphones and traveling into her musical realm.

7) Taking out a crossword puzzle that she can complete.

8) Rubbing her dog's belly and behind the dog's ears to listen to the contented sounds of an animal that feels cared for (sometimes when we don't feel cared for, the easiest thing to do to offer care to someone/something else.)

9) Taking out her Bible and reading an inspirational passage.

10) Taking a good look in the mirror and telling herself three good things about herself.

What is most important is that Nancy needs to DO something different to avoid sitting with these negative feelings. While there are some individuals who could simply sit, introspect and counteract their feelings without engaging in another activity, Nancy may not be able to do this. She must break the cycle of "I feel bad about myself; I wonder what I can find in the refrigerator/cupboard."

Once she has been successful in recognizing this script and changing it, it will get progressively easier. She will also start to believe that at least some of the time that she does NOT have to eat and can find another way in which to be happy with herself.

Is it likely that Nancy or YOU will change this behavior overnight and never lapse back into eating as a way to feel better? Of course not. However, the more nights she can avoid snack eating, the more faith she will develop in her long-term ability to stick with her weight loss commitment. Bear in mind too that Nancy may have some deeper work to do in order to confront her negative self-thinking altogether.

Teddy may have a bit more difficult time because his nail biting often takes place in his car while he is frantically driving somewhere. The long-term solution for Teddy probably involves more careful attention to his schedule. Chronically late people are often so task driven that the error they make is to try to get just one more thing done before they leave to go somewhere. Sometimes, they are overly optimistic about how long it will take to get to where they are going.

In the short run, Teddy can do the following to keep from tearing up his cuticles:

1) Using a three-sentence mantra that he could say to comfort himself: "Right now, I am not happy with myself. This feeling will pass quickly because I am going to arrive at my destination safely. Tomorrow is another day filled with opportunities for me to be on time."

2) Turning his favorite music up very loud.

3) Using a three-sentence mantra that he could say to comfort himself: "Right now, I am late. Although I am not thrilled with being late, I can listen to my latest book on the CD player.

4) Yelling or singing at the top of his lungs.

5) Filling his mouth with chewing gum, the more the better.

6) Taking out his electric razor and shaving again.

7) Calling someone on his hands-free car phone to chat.

8) Taking a drink from his cup of coffee.

9) Changing lanes safely several times.

10) Taking a good look in the mirror and telling himself three good things about himself (at full stops, of course).

Similarly to Nancy, Teddy needs to break the habit, in his case, of staring at his fingers when he is late. If he continues to focus on his fingers, he will invariably find a tiny area that requires "grooming." He needs instead to focus on the options that he has for doing something differently so that he experiences some success in overcoming his concerns about being late. In the long run, he will have to choose whether or not to adjust his timeliness. But that may not happen right away.

How will you be able set YOURSELF up to have immediate successes with YOUR issue? As you can see in the examples, finding as many options as possible will help you in the long run. On any given day, any one of those options may not do the trick. If you have enough fall back options to choose from, your chances of being successful are greater. If you only bring one option, you will likely fall back into old habits and scripts. Set yourself up (when you are not in crisis mode) to be successful by planning alternative behaviors for when you are in crisis mode. Then your brain will be more likely to think of possibilities when you need them most.

Chapter 16

YOUR ACTION PLAN

You've read about Cathy, Bruce, Nancy, Teddy and countless others. Maybe you thought that you could have easily dealt with their issues because they were EASY compared to YOUR issues. After all, YOUR issues are unique. No one has ever had issues like YOU have. Stop It. If their issues were solvable, it is possible that YOUR issues are solvable too.

All YOU need is that final push. You just need to leap before you look. Keeping your eyes focused on the prize is no easy task. As soon as you allow yourself to be distracted, it is easy to slide back into old scripts and behaviors. Remember that the payoffs you have for not changing our behavior are strong and can easily create images in your mind of pain to be avoided or a treacherous road ahead.

People who have been successful rising up from their hurt have found it helpful to create a written action plan that will help them stay on track. Below, you will find a template to help you do just that. Fill in the ACTION PLAN and get started changing your life TODAY.

MY ACTION PLAN

Prepare a separate ACTION PLAN for each issue YOU want to deal with. If you have several issues, pick the easiest one to solve first. That will give you momentum that YOU can later use to solve more complicated issues. Resist the temptation of solving the most important/toughest issue first. While logically sound, the odds of success are considerably lower than solving the easiest issue first.

READY? Let's get started.

There are 12 sections to your ACTION PLAN. Complete each section to help you stay on track.

SECTION #1: KNOW YOURSELF

Before you start to address your issue, it is important to understand how you reacted to the 7 elements described in Chapter 4. In that chapter, ideas were presented about how your brain perceives and reacts to hurtful events and memories. Feel free to reread the chapter so that you can answer these questions honestly.

Element #1

What is your "SELF CONCEPT?" Who are you? What matters most to you about the way you live your life on this planet?

_____

_____

_____

_____

_____

_____

Element #2

What is your pain tolerance? What kind of pain can you deal with? How do you deal with it? What is your preferred pain/pleasure ratio? (Remember that there is pain associated with growth, so suggesting that you want no pain will not be helpful in rising up from your hurt.

_____

_____

_____

_____

_____

Element #3

What payoffs drive you in general? Think of your deprivations. That may lead you to consider your daily motivations. What drives you?

_____

_____

_____

_____

_____

Element #4

How strong is your need for order, structure and consistency? How easy it for you to integrate new data, behaviors and concepts into what you believe? Will you have to change any other beliefs that you have in order to deal with this issue?

_____

_____

_____

_____

_____

Element #5

Do you desire closure and cognitive consistency whenever you integrate a new behavior? Does the new behavior have to fit with other elements of your life? Will the behavior change that YOU wish to make be dissonant or consonant with the way that you perceive yourself and the world around you? Do you seek closure that allows you the easiest path to emotional stability and contentment?

_____

_____

_____

_____

_____

_____

Element #6

Remember that this is an emotional event more than a logical event. Detailing how you FEEL will be critical to your success. Truly getting in touch with your FEARS, HURTS and other emotions will help you more than just logically thinking through the issue. What feelings are likely to come up during this transition?

_____

_____

_____

_____

_____

_____

Element #7

Remember that this process is about your IMPACTS more than it is about your INTENTS. I assume that YOU mean well as YOU start YOUR journey. That said, the impact of YOUR behaviors matter more. What impacts will you have to watch carefully?

_____

_____

_____

_____

_____

_____

SECTION #2: HOW HAVE YOU DEALT WITH YOUR HURT IN THE PAST?

Look at how you have handled hurtful situations in the past. You will consider 3 situations: Best Case Scenario, Worst Case Scenario and Most Probable Case Scenario. Remember that these can be about any hurtful situation you have encountered in the past, not necessarily the one you are focusing on here.

DESCRIBE A SITUATION WHERE YOU HAVE BEEN VERY SUCCESSFUL IN DEALING WITH YOUR HURT (BCS).

_____

_____

_____

_____

_____

_____

DESCRIBE A SITUATION WHERE YOU HAVE NOT BEEN AS SUCCESSFUL IN DEALING WITH YOUR HURT (WCS).

_____

_____

_____

_____

_____

_____

DESCRIBE HOW YOU HAVE TYPICALLY HANDLED YOUR HURT IN THE PAST

_____

_____

_____

_____

_____

_____

WHAT ARE THE SIMILARITIES AND DIFFERENCES BETWEEN THE WAYS IN WHICH YOU HAVE HANDLED YOUR HURT IN THE PAST?

_____
_____
_____
_____
_____
_____

SECTION #3: STATE THE ISSUE

Describe the issue you wish to focus on in several different ways or at several different levels.

Write down your first thoughts/description of your issue:

_____
_____
_____
_____
_____
_____

Now forget that and describe the issue in 2-3 other ways (looking at different elements or levels of the issue).

Alternative Issue Statement A

_____
_____
_____
_____
_____

Alternative Issue Statement B

_____
_____
_____
_____
_____

Alternative Issue Statement C

_____
_____
_____
_____
_____
_____

Which issue statement is the easiest to solve? Have you checked all of your assumptions? Have you attempted to "reframe" the issue back to the earliest, most accessible point of entry?

The issue statement I prefer to work with is ... because ...

_____
_____
_____
_____
_____
_____

SECTION#4: FEELINGS ABOUT THE ISSUE AND CAREFRONTATION

Identify the strongest feelings that you have concerning this issue. If possible, you can identify some of the "old scripts" that the feelings may be attached to. You will also identify what you will have to do to CAREFRONT the issue.

THE STRONGEST FEELINGS I HAVE WHEN DEALING WITH THIS ISSUE ARE:

_____
_____
_____
_____
_____
_____

THESE FEELINGS ARE ATTACHED TO SOME OF MY "OLD SCRIPTS" SUCH AS:

_____

_____

_____

_____

_____

_____

TO CAREFRONT THESE FEELINGS, IT WILL BE IMPORTANT TO:

_____

_____

_____

_____

_____

_____

WHAT WILL I DO TO CAREFRONT MY FEELINGS?

_____

_____

_____

_____

_____

_____

SECTION #5: PAYOFFS FOR NOT CHANGING

Consider all of the payoffs/benefits that you have for maintaining the status quo. Since you have chosen to deal with this issue in the same manner for a period of time, it is important to understand why. What benefits do you reap for not following through on making this decision?

THE PAYOFFS for NOT FIXING THIS ISSUE/RISING UP FROM HURT ARE:

1)

2)

3)

4)

5)

THE STRONGEST PAYOFF IS:

_____

If you can't/don't complete this section, you may not be looking at YOURSELF in a deep, honest and CAREFRONTIVE manner.

SECTION #6: PAYOFFS FOR CHANGING MY BEHAVIOR

Consider all of the benefits that you have for changing the status quo. Since you have chosen to deal with this issue at this time, what benefits will you reap from making a change?

The PAYOFFS for FIXING THIS ISSUE/RISING UP FROM HURT ARE:

1)

2)

3)

4)

5)

THE STRONGEST PAYOFF IS:

COMPARE YOUR FINAL ANSWER IN SECTIONS 5 AND 6. WHICH PAYOFF IS BETTER FOR YOUR SELF-CONCEPT?

SECTION #7: SENSE OF URGENCY

Consider how important it is for you to work on this issue NOW. After all of this time, why is NOW the perfect time to rise up from your hurt? What inspires you to face the pain and deal with issues head on? Why will this time be different?

_____

_____

_____

_____

_____

_____

SECTION #8: BEING STUCK AND GETTING UNSTUCK

Take a look at potential obstacles that can get in the way. What do you need to do to get yourself on the right track?

HAVE YOU BEEN STUCK IN YOUR BEHAVIOR? YES_____ NO_____

FOR HOW LONG? _____

WHAT ARE THE BIGGEST OBSTACLES IN YOUR WAY?

_____
_____
_____
_____
_____
_____

WHAT METHOD(S) WILL HELP YOU TO GET UNSTUCK?

_____
_____
_____
_____
_____
_____

SECTION #9: FACTORS TO USE IN EVALUATING YOUR OPTIONS

Consider the factors that are most important for you to use when looking at options to deal with your issue. Remember, you must decide how you will evaluate your options before you start to generate them. (If you don't remember the factors, please reread Chapter 12.)

How will you evaluate the options that you choose? What factors are of most significance to you as you make these changes in your life?

1)

2)

3)

4)

5)

Are some of these factors more important than other factors? Should you re-rank them or weight them according to their importance?

1)

2)

3)

4)

5)

WHICH FACTOR IS *THE* MOST IMPORTANT?

_____

SECTION # 10: OPTIONS, OPTIONS, OPTIONS

Identify at least 3-5 options for dealing with your issue.
What will YOU choose to DO to solve YOUR issue?

BEST CASE SCENARIO

_____

_____

_____

_____

_____

_____

WORST CASE SCENARIO

_____

_____

_____

_____

_____

_____

MOST PROBABLE CASE SCENARIO

_____

_____

_____

_____

_____

_____

Before you lock into any of those Options, what other Options might
YOU want to consider that are in between the Options Listed?

_____

_____

_____

_____

_____

_____

Thinking about which options are most likely to help you rise up from your hurt, list your 3 preferred options.

Plan A

_____

_____

_____

_____

_____

_____

Plan B

_____

_____

_____

_____

_____

Plan C

_____

_____

_____

_____

_____

_____

Remember that Option thinkers often think in terms of 5 options at the outset, but as long as YOU start with at least 3 Options, YOU'RE off to a great start.

SECTION #11: USING QUESTIONS TO REALITY TEST YOUR ASSUMPTIONS AND TO REFRAME THE ISSUE

Consider any assumptions that you are making that may hinder your progress. It is also important that you consider (for one last time), whether or not you are solving the issue at the most easily accessible point:

WHAT ASSUMPTIONS SHOULD BE REALITY TESTED?

_____
_____
_____
_____
_____
_____

WHAT QUESTIONS WILL YOU USE TO REALITY TEST THESE ASSUMPTIONS?

_____
_____
_____
_____
_____

DESCRIBE ANY EASIER ACCESS POINTS TO DEALING WITH THE SITUATION YOU ARE DESCRIBING:

_____
_____
_____
_____
_____
_____

SECTION #12: OVERCOMING FEAR OF FAILURE (FOF) BY USING SSPS (SUCCESSFUL SEQUENTIAL PROBLEM SOLVING)

Identify the first three steps YOU will take that will start YOU off on the path to success. Make sure that the steps are easy and that they are likely to be successful. That will provide momentum to overcome FOF (Fear of Failure). You will also consider how to continue the new behavior in the long run.

Step # 1:

_____
_____
_____
_____
_____
_____

Step #2:

_____
_____
_____
_____
_____

Step #3:

_____
_____
_____
_____
_____

Now let's take a slightly longer view. How will YOU keep on YOUR PATH it in the long term?

_____

_____

_____

_____

_____

_____

How does it feel to have a plan that is going to work for YOU?

_____

_____

_____

_____

_____

It's time to stop reading and time to GET STARTED!!!

Chapter 17

STAYING ON TRACK

OK, you have gotten started. Now you are beginning to ask yourself if you are off to a good start. That is a fair question. What does a good start look and feel like? How will you recognize it?

Let me start by describing what other folks have considered a good start. Many people feel great pride after the first week of a new behavior. Others wait two weeks before allowing themselves to celebrate. While you are different and unique, it is important to recognize, acknowledge and appreciate any initial success that you are having.

Just getting into motion after a long period of inertia usually feels terrific. The very idea that you are "at least doing *something*" is a refreshing feeling. You may feel that you are ready to turn the corner. After a long period of paralyzing inactivity in relation to your issue, being in motion feels very liberating and exciting. Almost euphoric.

As I stated earlier, initial successes should be noted and celebrated. While it may not be time for a full parade and statue just yet, it is important to acknowledge yourself and your good start. Many people, after reading this book, have never gotten that far.

Starting a journal to write down your progress and how you feel is a great way to celebrate each success and challenge along the way. If you are open and can articulate your feelings daily, you will have a written record of what you did and how you felt about it. Rereading your entries later may reinforce and strengthen you to continue on your chosen path when times get tougher.

Patting yourself on the back is another good idea. You may be the only person to really recognize or care about your progress. Hearing you cheer for yourself could bring a smile to your face.

Allowing yourself a treat is also a good idea unless it involves repeating your old behavior. Having a drink when you are trying to stop drinking won't help. Placing a bet when you are trying to stop gambling isn't the kind of treat I had in mind.

Symbolic treats may be more powerful than physical treats. Honoring yourself by creating a certificate of merit could be fun. How about taking a picture of yourself smiling and putting it up on your bathroom mirror? How about creating a PMA (positive mental attitude) mantra to repeat to yourself as your success grows?

"I have made progress in developing my ability to _____. I have been successful yesterday and today. I am going to be successful tomorrow too. I am well on my way to becoming a new and better person."

While I want you to celebrate your initial successes, I want you to use additional tools to help you stay on track as time progresses. As you progress, you can periodically use different types of "feedback" to reality test how successful you are.

Three categories of "feedback" that may be helpful to use are:
1) Feedback from other people around you
2) Feedback from your body and
3) Feedback from your mind (emotional and logical).

Talking to your support group, family, friends and/or professionals about your progress may elicit kind words, thoughts and encouragement. It can also provide suggestions to further hone your new behavior if you are open to hearing them.

That is the critical issue about feedback. How open are you to listen to others (or even yourself)? If one person gives you feedback about a particular issue, it may be a statement about YOU or them. If two people give you the same feedback, there might be a theme here. When three or more people tell YOU the same thing, it's probably time to listen.

The feedback you will receive will depend on who you ask, how you ask for it and what you ask.

Who should you ask?

Feedback will be more valuable when individuals:
1) Truly care about you
2) Are trusted insofar as having offered you sage advice or comments in the past

3) Are objective and will not let their feelings for you color the accuracy and veracity of their observations

4) Are around enough to be able to observe your behavior at least several times

5) Are articulate in their observations and

6) Want to be of help to you and feel comfortable giving you feedback.

That said, stay away from "naysayers" and negative Nellies at this point. The last thing you need to hear someone tell you is "Big Deal, you've gotten started and then failed before. Let's see if you can stick to it this time." Even if this is true, it is not likely to help you stay on the path. It is not constructive feedback.

There is a big difference between constructive and destructive feedback. Constructive feedback is given with caring (as with all CAREFRONTATION.) The intention and impact is to help the receiver. It is not at all centered on the giver. Destructive feedback is more like a confrontation in that it is aggressive. While the intention may not be to hurt the receiver, the impact may still hurt. Sometimes, it is as much of a statement about the giver as it is about the receiver.

How should you ask them for feedback?

That sounds like a simple and straightforward process, so compare the following two approaches:

A) Mark, I am in the midst of trying to do something different about my issue of _____. Since I am very close to the issue, I would like to get an outside opinion on how it looks to another person. Would you be willing to help me?

B) Mark, you are a person that I respect. I value your opinion and have benefitted in the past from some of your comments and observations about my behavior. I am engaged in a personal growth activity where I am going to develop a better way of handling my issue of _____. I could really use your help in staying on track. Would you be willing to help me to SUCCEED by giving me feedback?

The second approach is much more empathic and may be more likely to get honest and straightforward feedback. However, you know the potential feedback givers, their styles and comfort levels, so ask each person in a way that is natural to you and them.

You are most likely to get good feedback when you:
1) Ask in a sincere manner
2) Emphasize that receiving feedback is important to you
3) Tell them you value their feedback
4) Appreciate their time and effort.

How many people should you ask for feedback?

If you can handle it, I would recommend at least 3 people (or some other odd number.) In this way, there can at least be a majority opinion. Remember, as with all activities associated with option thinking, the more options considered, the better the result.

What should you ask for feedback about? This is an important issue. Do not just ask for feedback ONLY about the behavior you are changing. While that is important, it may be equally important to get feedback about how you are behaving in other ways and in other situations. Coping with a problem may cause you to exaggerate behaviors in seemingly non-related activities (e.g., you might have a shorter fuse during frustrating situations). That would be good information to have.

Feedback about your physical appearance, your general mood, your overall attitude or how often you are smiling, sad or angry might also be valuable for you. Feedback about these issues may allow you to calibrate how much energy and effort it is taking for you to establish your new behavior.

Evaluating Feedback

Writing down as much of the feedback as possible is another good idea. When you initially hear feedback, you may become very defensive and want to argue against the feedback. You may not even hear it accurately because you perceive it as threatening. If you write down what you have heard, you can reread it several days later when you may be calmer or have a different perspective about it. You can also go back to the person who gave the feedback with questions about it if you are not sure what they meant or want a specific example. You can compare feedback at different points in time to see if the feedback is consistent, similar or different.

If the feedback you are getting from others is positive and matches your own perception, that is a good sign. This is not a guarantee that things will work out well, but it does increase your chances of success. If there are minor variances here, you can choose whether or not to accept the feedback as offered. You can ask yourself whether or not fine tuning is required.

If the feedback you are receiving varies greatly from your own perception, this may be a good time to take a "time out" and reflect on what is going on. Ask other people to explain why they feel the way they do. Ask for evidence or specific examples that you can review and consider. Resist the temptation of arguing or debating with the feedback givers. It is not a debate and no points are given for "winning" or "proving them wrong."

The best thing you can do is to suspend judgment for a few days. Let their words wash over you. Mull over what they are saying without deciding whether it is true or not or whether or not you believe and accept it. Feedback may be perceived differently after some time has gone by.

Receiving negative feedback does not mean that you are wrong or failing. But it does mean that you may wish to reconsider the option you have chosen. You may also ask other people for feedback to see if more people around you feel the same way. It should at least give you pause. You may also want to look at the 2 other levels of feedback to see if there are other indicators that things are not going as planned.

Providing Feedback to Yourself

The second layer of feedback is derived from observing things about yourself. It is important to check in with your own body and to view related behaviors. Your body will seek a homeostatic state where there is stability and structure in how you deal with day-to-day activities and events.

When an UNBALANCED FORCE is added to the equation, you can be thrown out of equilibrium. Here are a few areas to observe for changes:
1) Sleeping behavior including total time slept, how often you awaken during the night, use of the restroom during the night, nightmares, sleep walking, sleep talking

2) Eating and Drinking behavior including how much food/drink you are consuming and what type of food/drink you are consuming, particularly if it varies dramatically from your typical diet

3) Bathroom behavior in terms of frequency, regularity and unusual occurrences

4) Physical appearance in terms of tiredness, sluggishness, animation or other changes

5) Concern for personal appearance (which can be heightened or lessened)

6) Social interactions in terms of frequency, interest and types of events and people involved

7) Exaggerations of personality characteristics such as unusual bursts of anger or hurt, quietness, withdrawal

8) Forgetfulness and an increased number of errors at work or at home

9) Changes in personal style, values, morals or attitudes

10) Energy Level which can be dramatically higher or lower

11) High levels of boredom

12) Vacillation or indecision over important matters

13) Preoccupation with relatively trivial issues

14) Inattentiveness and inability to concentrate

15) Irritability

16) Excessive procrastination

17) Unexplained dissatisfaction

18) Accident proneness

19) Lower levels of trust of others

20) General disorganization

21) Role confusion

22) Restlessness

23) Development of allergic reactions

24) Change in weight

25) Atypical behaviors of any kind.

If this list of symptoms seems familiar, it should. Many of these behavioral changes are symptoms of general stress. Stress (which can be positive or negative) occurs when you are thrown out of equilibrium.

Sometimes making a positive change can throw another aspect of your life out of balance. It is important to take a physical and emotional inventory periodically to see if this is happening.

If there are no or relatively few changes in these behaviors, it means that you are adjusting to the changes that you are making in a positive manner. Your mind and body have no need to compensate or change other behaviors in response to your new way of being. That is a good sign.

If, however, there are other changes that you notice, this does not mean that you should discontinue new behaviors. It does mean that you should look carefully at how fast you are moving and consider fine tuning adjustments.

Bringing the Feedback Together

Compare your observations of body and mood changes to the feedback you have received from other people. Hopefully, there is consistency in the feedback. If there is relative inconsistency, at some point you will have to decide which feedback to value higher. You may also want to evaluate the third and last level of feedback.

Perhaps the most important feedback that you need is from taking a good, honest look at yourself. Only you know exactly the journey that you are on. Only you know if you are really doing what you claim to be doing. Remember, at the beginning of this process, I suggested to you that YOU must be honest with yourself about what you are and aren't doing. That is one of tent poles to the entire process. Spending times introspecting about your "SELF CONCEPT" and your payoffs will serve you well. Having a clear picture of who you are today and who you would like to become in the future is a strong barometer to use when measuring your progress.

When the Going Gets Tough

There will be constant internal dialogue about payoffs for keeping the issue versus payoffs for getting rid of the issue. This internal dialogue will show up in your dreams, conscious and unconscious thought processes. When you feel that it is just too hard to keep going or you aren't making progress fast enough, it will help you to understand that psychological defense mechanisms can easily take you off track.

When you feel ready to give the journey up, ask yourself if this is really how you feel. It may be a reflection of your mind's anticipation of exaggerated unknown future possible pain. Once you imagine how painful it could be, a variety of "good reasons" may occur to you to abandon the process. After all, in the short run, it is usually easier to revert back to old ways than to proceed. You will have to be especially vigilant during this phase.

You may find it necessary to recommit yourself to the journey many times. Each time, you may have to go back to the beginning of the process and make another decision to continue. Don't be discouraged by this. It is typical, and each time you have to do it, it will take less time. Each time you go through this process, it will keep you grounded and in the long run, it will increase your chances of being successful.

You may be concerned with how you are doing compared to others. You may wonder if other people make regular continuous linear progress. Rarely. Often, it is two steps forward, one step backwards. Sometimes, you work at it for a while, and then take a rest. Be careful because inertia can settle back in very quickly.

As soon as you realize that you have taken a "mini-vacation" from your journey, it is time to re-pack your bags, re-fortify your commitment and start again. Relapses are common and expected in the early phases of behavior change. However, because you have let your guard down for a time or two does not mean that you will not succeed. Real behavior change is not usually even a possibility until after the first month or so.

Remember too that it is not whether or not you relapse, or even for how long you relapse, as much as it is about what you do AFTER you relapse. It is easy for a sad mood to overcome you when you relate the current temporary return to old behavior to previous failed attempts to change your life. If you accept that perspective, it can become a "self-fulfilling prophecy." Better to pick yourself up, dust yourself off, and renew your commitment.

At this point, rereading your journal of early progress, asking for support from your support group, friends, family or sponsors can help. If they are accepting, non-judgmental people, they will understand the true difficulty of the journey. They may share with you the number of times they relapsed back into old behavior before they were finally able to commit to more permanent behavior change. People are rarely perfect in their journey. If it took you five, ten or twenty years to dig yourself into a hole, why would you expect to climb out the first time you try?

That is why there is a need to reality test your perceptions of how you are doing. That is why asking for and receiving feedback matters. If you never document your progress in a journal and never tell anyone what you are attempting to do, you only have your own perceptions as the "official barometer" for how you are doing. Even the most objective people don't always realize when they are wearing "rose colored glasses."

You must maintain a sense of urgency about completing the task. Understanding how important it is to stay on track may only come AFTER the change has been made and set into your behavior. In retrospect, YOU may look back and wonder why it took you so long to get started. You will wonder how you could have lived with the issue for as long as you did. Don't seek to put everything into perspective yet. That will occur in time.

The bottom line to all of this is fairly simple. Are you happy/happier than you were before? Is the issue that was robbing you of time, energy, happiness or money getting easier to handle? Do you sense the freedom and opportunities that life without this issue can provide?

Chapter 18

THE REST OF YOUR LIFE

Congratulations! If you have read this far, you know what it will take to rise up from your hurt. Hopefully, you are motivated and chomping at the bit to put everything you've learned in this book into motion and change your life. Maybe you have already done so with one or two issues. Maybe you have already become your own UNBALANCED FORCE that resists the return to inertia and keeps you in continuous motion.

Whether or not you have initiated action YET is not critical, as long as you realize that change is the grand theme of this book. Changing your entire life. Change is not limited to solving your current issue; it can serve as a guide to dealing with the rest of your time on this planet.

The journey of your life is filled with problems and hurdles. Hopefully, it is also filled with joy and wonder. That is what makes the journey so fascinating. You can be progressing along your merry way when suddenly a troubling issue crops up. Conversely, you can be mired in the midst of a draining issue and find yourself amazed at the beauty of a warm fall day. You never know what each day will bring.

However, when you have the ability to deal effectively with whatever each day brings, you at least "perceive" that you have more control in your life. Perception matters. Once you perceive that you are strong enough, not only to survive, but to thrive, there isn't that much that can be intimidating to you. You become an increasingly resilient person, a person who always believes that you can prevail. That type and amount of confidence becomes apparent to you and to the people around you.

While you can't always control the twists and turns of your life, you can usually control your reactions to those twists and turns. If you believe that you can find a strategy that will allow you to make the best of the situation or rise over the temporary hurdle that currently confronts you,

you will have more confidence about taking action. This kind of resilience can serve to lengthen the quantity and quality of the days of your life.

When you make a life-long commitment to face the problems that come your way, you take the stance that you are ready, willing and able to stand tall. You can look back at your life to this point and see how you shied away from such direct confrontations previously. It is reassuring to now know that you have the tools, experience and hopefully some success in facing issues to fall back on.

Does this mean that you will never slide back into old behaviors? No. But it does mean that when you do, you will be able to recognize it, be able to understand how and why it happened and have the ability to get back on the right track again. Once you understand your payoff structure and your reactions to pain, it becomes harder to fool yourself into thinking that there isn't anything you can't do.

Let's face it. This book, like any other self-help book, is not a panacea that will guarantee a smile on your face every day. There are certain issues that must be grieved and processed before you can step into dealing with them more fully. You are a human being, and old ways can be seductive.

Now, however, relapses and/or temporary setbacks can be viewed for what they are: Temporary. Not total failures or lifelong sentences to misery.

Remember Cathy? Once she chose to redefine who she was as a mother, spouse and teacher, her whole world opened up for her. Not only did she have more time for herself, but she actually enhanced the lives of her children, husband and students by expecting them to learn to take more care of themselves. Was there a rough adjustment patch where she had her doubts? Was there a period of time when she was questioned and challenged by her children, spouse and students? Sure. But that is how growth happens. Through temporary conflict that is resolved in a positive fashion.

And what about Bruce? Once he started to communicate about how he was feeling to Emily, he wasn't confronting all of his issues alone any more. Emily was able to relate. Bruce started to reach out to people in his environment as friends and slowly found FUN entering his life again without resorting to the "16-ounce lift" he did at the bar. He no longer needed to fantasize about younger women. Discussions about intimacy recharged his passion for Emily, who provided compassion, understanding and energy in every room of their house.

Did each person mentioned in this book turn his or her life around? Hardly. Maybe if this was a Disney movie, everyone would live happily ever after. But this isn't a movie. It is real life filled with tough choices and no guarantees. In real life, you don't get what you deserve. Sometimes you just get what you get, but, more than sometimes, you get what you are able to create for yourself.

How will it turn out for YOU? Will YOU become one of the people who change his/her life? Or will YOU seek the next self-help book? The next guru?

I know many people who are forever seeking to "understand" their issue first and then deal with it after that. While that is an interesting idea in theory, understanding at a deep level usually occurs after the actual resolution of the issue. Only when you have had some distance from the issue, been able to compare old and new payoffs, can you really understand how all of the pieces fit together.

It is now time to act, time to turn the corner in your life, time to make a new beginning. A beginning where you are creating your own future rather than just reacting to what others do. It is time for you to breathe the fresh air that comes to you when you march toward each new day with the confidence, tools and ability to truly "Seize The Day."

A wise teacher of mine once said that the true value of a teacher is not that he/she imparts what she/he knows to the students. It is that the teacher motivates the students to go far beyond what the teacher ever considered. To stretch the boundaries/options further than they had been stretched before.

In that vein, I want to give you encouragement not only to rise up from hurt in your own life but to offer inspiration to other people that you know and work with. There are others in your family and your place of business who could benefit from an acceleration and impetus to change their lives as well. Life is short, and each day that passes with unresolved issues is lost and can never be fully recovered.

Don't waste another moment.

Today is the first day of the rest of your life, and it is time to live the life that you want and deserve.

I hope that I have been able to serve as part of the UNBALANCED FORCE that changes your life.

Humbly,

Dr. Tom Steiner

Alpha Coach

January 2017

Printed in the United States
By Bookmasters